Bridge Over Troubled Water

To my good friend
John and his family
with my best wishes.

17-3-95.

BRIDGE OVER TROUBLED WATER

An insight into the English-Speaking Union and its influence in South Asia

MICHAEL WYNNE-PARKER

Kingston Books

ISBN 0-9514937-0-1
Published by Kingston Books Ltd,
5A Hurdwick Place, Hampstead Road,
London NW1 2JE.

Designed by Peter Dolton.
Design and production in association with
Book Production Consultants, 47 Norfolk Street, Cambridge.
Typeset by Cambridge Photosetting Services.
Printed and bound by Bookcraft (Bath) Ltd,
Midsomer Norton, Avon.

To Jennie, Sarah and Fiona
and my many friends in South Asia

ACKNOWLEDGEMENTS

I acknowledge with gratitude a great deal of help from a number of people, especially Lynn Boyo, Rebecca Vincent-Smith and Jean Huse (research); Elaine Morris (typing); Valerie Mitchell (London launch); and my long-suffering publishers, David Benedictus and Karen Ross, at Kingston Books.

CONTENTS

PREFACE

Brought up to an Empire being cast away and the *Pax Britannica* fading into regional warfare, I had a dream that one day . . . But history seldom repeats itself and the dream, already a reality, was taking a different course. The world was avidly reading English.

My mother tongue had become my country's secret weapon and, as an author, I was heir to a priceless birthright.

The ESU is very much a part of what might be described as the 'English explosion' that has taken place as a result of World War II and the need for a *lingua-franca* to ease the flow of air traffic, shipping and world trade. But very few of its members know much about its origins or its overseas potential.

This very readable, and at times almost racy book is in part a biography of the Union's founder, and in part a glimpse of how a few dedicated people are widening the Union's scope, particularly in Southern Asia.

We are fortunate in having a man of Michael Wynne-Parker's talent and energy, something that is very apparent in the quick-fire thumbnail sketch of himself he gives at the outset. He is not only a good fund-raiser and organiser, but a very good communicator. A compulsive and fascinating talker, it is only now, after all the years I have known him, that I have discovered he is also a good writer.

I commend this book to all my fellow members of the English-Speaking Union – the perfect gift to increase membership of an organisation bent on promoting our most important asset.

It is, after all, by words that man communicates his ideas.

Hammond Innes

INTRODUCTION

A foreword by Dr. T.P. Amerasinghe, President, English-Speaking Union of Sri Lanka

"There's a divinity that shapes our ends,
Rough-hew them how we will"

Hamlet

My chance meeting with the author of this book led to a whole chain of events – not least, the development of English teaching in Sri Lanka and throughout South Asia. It was just such a meeting between Sir Evelyn Wrench and Charles Cochrane in a London cafe in 1912 that led to the formation of the English-Speaking Union of the Commonwealth in 1917.

Indeed, chance has played a great part in Sri Lanka's association with Britain in recorded history. In the 1st Century A.D., when Roman arms subjugated British tribes south of the 'borders', Pliny records that a Sri Lankan Ambassador named Racchia sat with Emperor Claudius on the purple throne of the Caesars at the trial of several captive princes soon to be thrown over the Tarpeian Rock. The story may be apocryphal, but it seems that Racchia saved the life of Caractacus – the first occasion in Roman history when a rebel received the imperial pardon!

The same chance or divinity, centuries later, saw the ignominious defeat of Lord North's British Army in Kandy, in 1801, about the time of Trafalgar and the Battle of the Nile. This led to the Kandyan Convention of 1815, which in effect was not a treaty of subjugation but an exchange of Kings – George III of England for Sri Wickrema Rajasinghe of the Sinhalese.

In 1948, after almost another 150 years of war, conquest and development, Kandy was the scene of another historic meeting. At the Octagonal of the Temple of the Tooth, the Union Jack gave way to the flag of the rampant lion in an atmosphere of goodwill. As equal partners under the Statute of Westminster, Sri Lanka and Britain exemplified the truth of Kipling's lines:

> *"But there is neither East nor West, Border nor Breed,*
> *nor Birth*
> *When two strong men stand face to face,*
> *though they come from the ends of the earth!"*

And so to 1983, when Margaret Thatcher met J. R. Jayawardene; the British Prime Minister and the Sri Lankan President, in the central hills of Sri Lanka, to inaugurate Britain's historic gift – the Victoria Dam. Shades of Shakespeare, the "Sweet Swan of Avon", floated in the waters of the man-made lake as Mrs. Thatcher recalled old Polonius's advice to his son Laertes:

> *"The friends thou hast, and their adoption tried,*
> *Grapple them to thy soul with hoops of steel."*

Great minds think alike. The Sri Lankan President had quoted the lines a year earlier, when he had reminded the U.K. Government that a treaty of mutual military assistance still existed, despite Sri Lanka's independent status.

In the cultural field, the same fortuitous circumstances bind the English language and its vicissitudes – the subject of Michael Wynne-Parker's book – with Sri Lanka. With the conquest of the Maritime Provinces and the subjugation of the Highlands of Kandy, King Emperor's English was imposed on the people.

As the early British educationalist Charles Grant commented: "To introduce the language of the conquerors seems to be an obvious means of assimilating the conquered people to them."

Lord Macauley's Minute of 1835 set the seal on the educational pattern adopted by Britain in her Asian colonies. It led to a misguided attempt to give an 'English' mind to subject people and succeeded only in producing caricatures. It was not surprising, therefore, when the nations of South Asia obtained their independence, that the abolition of English became the popular cry.

English was formally dethroned in Sri Lanka in 1956, with mixed consequences. The Sinhala language developed, but the attendant evils were great. Whole generations were denied a knowledge of English at a time when increasingly in the post-war period it became the language of science, law, diplomacy and commerce. It was a tragedy that just as English was taking an upward swing, Sri Lanka decided to downgrade it. It is now universally agreed that many of Sri Lanka's present troubles stem from this unfortunate revolution; if the water in the bath had to be thrown away, the baby might have been preserved!

Much more recently, with the Thirteenth Amendment to the Constitution, English came into its own in Sri Lanka. As Michael Wynne-Parker points out, it has come back not as King Emperor's English or Queen's English, but as a 'servant' language with many masters. 'Servant' is not used in any derogatory sense; the word recognises the functional importance of English. As Richard Francis, Director General of the British Council, has said: "As a language which 'other people' speak, English is unrivalled; its functional power is unassailable. It is currency against which all others are measured – the gold standard of international connection."

It is this English which has been ennobled; King Emperor's English was trodden underfoot, then re-moulded into shape. Throughout South Asia, it has come to be recognised as 'currency' more valuable than bank notes for the quantity it can buy. The purchases are valuable goods in the form of technological development, trade exchanges, access to information and research, the pleasures of British literature and art. What is more, it is a currency which appreciates in value.

It is also a standard of measurement. As the Sri Lankan Minister of Education, Culture and Information, the Hon. W. J. M. Lokubandara has recently said: "Whether in the administration, the private sector, higher education or elsewhere, the persons with fluency in English are the ones who get the best deal. The unfortunate masses who are discriminated against by this dominant position of English receive step-motherly treatment. The average person refers to English as Kaduwa, meaning sword. My aim is to make this weapon available to all classes. The English language is the weapon by which the upper classes control the masses. What is important is to break the monopoly that the upper classes have with English and to make it available to the people at large."

Michael Wynne-Parker's book breaks new ground in this direction. It points the way to quenching the great new thirst for English now sweeping the sub-continent. At this moment of decision, the vehicle has presented itself largely due to his efforts within the English-Speaking Union and its South Asia Council. These efforts are reminiscent of Sir Evelyn Wrench's efforts in the years between the great wars. Then, as an Anglo-American collaboration, the ESU proved its usefulness. Sir Winston Churchill referred to how the new world came to the defence of the old and described the part played by the English-Speaking Union in encouraging that timely intervention.

Today, we have another Sir Evelyn, in the author of this book.

Michael Wynne-Parker has a keen perception of the new role the English-Speaking Union has to play. He knows that in the not-too-distant future, the old world will have to come to the defence of the new. The British public will need to be fully involved. For the Commonwealth itself, English is a powerful cohesive force. The need for a Commonwealth University is paramount. It is England's task to help member countries maintain and develop levels of competence in English as a key to economic development.

The author is positive that England cannot and should not leave the demand for English in Asia or Africa – or, for that matter in any part of the world – unattended. He is equally positive that the British public should not leave it in the hands of government alone; he knows the temper of South Asia. Despite its record of good work in this direction, the British Council has not yet impinged upon the masses. Therefore, Mr. Wynne-Parker urges the English-Speaking Union of the Commonwealth and its International Council to take a big hand because, as a people's movement, its motives cannot be called into question.

As the pages of 'Bridge Over Troubled Water' unfold, we see a man with an abiding interest in Sri Lanka, its people and – through them – all South Asia. In the grand tradition of other Englishmen of the past, he spares no pains in his crusade to make English available to the masses.

Time, money and hard work are of little significance in his endeavours. Not content with Sri Lanka, his chosen territory, he has travelled with me to the landlocked kingdom of the Himalayas, to Nepal, to the many-splendoured isles of the Maldives and throughout India either to set up new ESU branches or to resuscitate those established years ago. It is an understatement to say that his enthusiasm is infectious. Presidents, Prime Ministers and educationalists in South Asia are his friends and associates in the supremely important task of making English available to the man in the street, thus releasing him from the bondage of the colonial past.

To sum up, Michael Wynne-Parker's book is the answer to the prophetic question posed by the English poet Samuel Daniel:

INTRODUCTION

"And who, in time, knows whither we may vent
The treasure of our tongue, to what strange shores
This gain of our best glory shall be sent,
T'enrich unknowing nations with our stores?
What worlds in th' yet unreformed Occident
May come refin'd with th'accents that are ours."

Dr. T. P. Amerasinghe
Colombo, Sri Lanka
July 1989

Chapter 1

BEGINNINGS

"I pray that you may be
As steadfast as a tree,
Putting on thoughts like leaves
That grace the spring;
That, waking or asleep,
Your roots may quarry deep
Into the lovely heart
Of everything.

I pray that you may be
As graceful as a tree,
Noble and pure in thought,
And word and deed;
As lovely as the pine,
Superb in every line,
Whether the storm or sun
May meet her need.

I pray that you may grow
Until men come to know
Truth in your life and wisdom
In your eyes.
God grant that you may be
As steadfast as a tree
That lifts her lovely life towards
The open skies."

Friendships Prayer
Derek Neville

From every book one learns something of its author. And when one has been inspired by a book, it is only natural to wish to meet the source of that inspiration.

It seemed fortuitous then that when I first went to live in Norfolk, I discovered that I was going to have Derek Neville as a near neighbour. For some years I had greatly admired Neville's poems and short stories, although in other ways we had little in common. I made myself known to him to find that he had a slightly eastern European look, to which no doubt his greying beard contributed. He was running a small restaurant at Itteringham Mill. The food was rather too healthy for my taste, but we sat in his huge library and talked about poetry, and when I left, I bought copies of all his available books.

It was an unusual friendship, I suppose, because in many ways we were so opposed. I have always been interested in field sports; Derek was a vegetarian. I had been greatly influenced by Anglo-Catholicism; Derek's religion was a kind of pantheism. Certainly, he disliked established religions.

Some years later my wife, Jennie, and I received an invitation at unusually short notice to dine with him and his wife, Mary. It was a perfect early summer's evening, and when we arrived we had a drink – at least Jennie and I did, for Derek was teetotal – and were shown into a most attractive private room where the table had been set for two. Derek announced that we could talk later, and somewhat to our surprise left us! A waitress served us dinner, which was delicious although eaten mainly in silence, and it was only after the coffee, when we were invited into the *sanctum sanctorum* – the library – that I discovered what had been behind the invitation.

"You know," he said, "you're a young man, and I feel you have a challenging future. You will, I think, greatly contribute to a cause of international significance."

It was at this point that he mentioned that he had to give me a 'message from Goethe' and wrote out on the back of an envelope the following:

> *What you can do – or think you can – Begin it!*
> *Boldness hath genius, power and magic in it.*
> *Only engage, and then the mind grows heated*
> *Begin!*
> *And soon your task shall be completed.*

I put the envelope in my wallet, feeling more than a little over-awed, and went home. Within a few days both Derek and Mary had died from natural causes. I looked again at the back of the envelope. It now seemed like a challenge from beyond the grave.

At the very least I felt greatly encouraged to devote more time and energy to an organisation I somehow seemed to have drifted into. That organisation was the English-Speaking Union.

Chapter 2

ORIGINS

" 'Tis virtue, and not birth that makes us noble:
Great actions speak great minds, and such should govern."

The Prophetess
Beaumont & Fletcher

My father died in an accident when I was ten. Sadly, I remember very little about him. His claim to fame is that he had helped to set up and run the Blood Transfusion Service. My mother was a nurse, and they met when he was in hospital receiving treatment for tuberculosis. After they married they lived in Derbyshire, the county from which my mother came and in which I was born, despite my long Welsh ancestory.

After my father's death we were plunged into financial straits, and my mother was reduced to taking in lodgers. One of these lodgers was a military man, whom my mother later married. I shall never forget the first time I met him, because he had had his arm blown off in the war.

My schooldays were uninspiring and I think I might have been described as a below-average student! Only recently have I thought how irrelevant much of what I was taught has been in my adult life. I was poor at mathematics, yet I was to find myself responsible for millions of pounds when I became an investment manager.

It was while I was at school that I became religiously inclined and learned to love rituals in all their forms.. I was especially attracted to Anglo-Catholicism with its colourful vestments, incense, music and order. I flirted with Roman Catholicism – not unknown in our family – and was attracted by its apparent mysticism and the beauty of the Latin Mass. Alas, both Anglicans and Romans have stripped their services of much glorious ritual, and much inspiring language has been replaced by the mundane.

I left school in my late teens with enough money from a trust to keep me going for about ten years. I got through it all by the time I was thirty.

This is not the place to relate in detail those ten formative years in my university of life. My interest in religion, however, continued.

I dabbled with the Billy Graham movement, but rejected it because I was suspicious of its fundamentalist naivety. I took a correspondence course in comparative religions and went so far as to learn Greek so that I could read the Bible in that language. I even tried to learn Hebrew, but, without a natural talent for languages, it was an uphill struggle.

I travelled. I can't remember the time when I haven't had the ambition to travel. I travelled almost everywhere.

My first overseas journey was to New York, where, at the age of 20, I had gone to find some Wynne cousins. I had the extraordinary good fortune to stumble across a White Russian called Andres Mendoza, and he in turn introduced me to one or two ageing but flamboyant characters, like Sergei Obolinsky, who performed a dagger dance for me on the tables at the Waldorf-Astoria. My fascination for ritual was further fired when my White Russian friends took me for the first time to a Russian Orthodox church. Not that it was a church, so much as a converted ballroom in a house belonging to the Russians. No sooner had I heard – and seen – the Slavonic liturgy, than I decided that perhaps this was for me.

As a city I found New York initially unfriendly – I was to discover years later that Sir Evelyn Wrench, founder of the English-Speaking Union, reacted to New York in just the same way on his first visit – but I quickly learned the lesson all travellers need to learn, that it is not places but people that charm you. Also that for most Englishmen, America is an acquired taste. In the course of several visits, I travelled from

Florida to Alaska, from California to New England. I felt then as the Pilgrim Fathers must have felt as they beached their flimsy craft; this was a land of opportunity if you dared to take the chance.

I was no colonist however. Had I been so, Virginia would have been the state in which I would have most liked to make my home. Years later I did stay in Richmond, Virginia, on English-Speaking Union business. My host was an estimable German, about 80, named Edward von Selzan. He had been a junior diplomat in Holland at the outbreak of the war, and had refused to permit Hitler's photograph to sully the walls of his office. He was warned that if it was not in place by the end of the day he would be in hot water, so he escaped to the States and set about selling life assurance, which I too have sold in my time. He was successful and flourished.

The house was truly remarkable. Every niche, every shelf, every surface was crammed with piles of journals, magazines and books, all meticulously arranged. The house was also crammed with pretty girls, and I formed the impression that he was shortly to marry one of them.

Over dinner he told me about his truly illustrious neighbour, the Crown Princess Anastasia, thought by some to be the long-lost daughter of the Tsar. I had always had an amateur interest in and a healthy respect for history – the more romantic the better – so I plucked up the courage to ask, might I visit her? He made a telephone call to her new husband, Professor John Manahan, and an appointment was confirmed. I was warned that a wait of two hours to see the Princess was commonplace, and that Maria Rasputin whose father had been responsible for the ultimate downfall of the Romanovs, had been kept waiting for two days.

However, it was not long before there was a knocking at an upstairs window and I was taken down to the basement at the foot of a flight of stairs. At the top of the stairs appeared a little old woman with white, untidy hair above a pale countenance. She said a few words in German and then there was the screech of a cat and she disappeared. That was my brief audience with Anastasia. I don't know and shall never know whether I had been standing in the presence of one of the most remarkable women of the century, or a splendid and glorious imposter.

I first travelled to the Middle East in the late sixties. Unlike America, it was not the heat that made an overwhelming impression on me there (it may have been hotter than Philadelphia, but it didn't seem to be), it was the antiquity of the ancient civilisations. Here, stretched out before me, was what I had merely read and dreamed about as a child. Actually to arrive in that ancient place filled me with a strange sense of optimism and excitement. Everything that happened to us had happened before – probably many times before.

Although on that first visit I was a tourist, I was certainly a privileged one. I had met King Hussein of Jordan in London and had an invitation to visit his palace in Amman, and to stay in his house in East Jerusalem. In those days of course, the Old City was still a part of Jordan, and my only experience of Israel was from across the border.

On my second visit I arrived on the first day of the Six Day War. I was at a reception in the ruins of King David's Palace when there was a vast – and to all of us – totally inexplicable explosion. I found myself blown straight into the arms of the Bishop of Mexico.

He said: "I've got a car here," and gave me a lift to the King David Hotel. Although the soldiers were impressed by his Bishop's attire, we still had to show our passports. We were to spend that night under the table in the hotel, which of course had been bombed too, wondering what the hell was going to happen next.

It was my first experience of war conditions, of seeing people murdering each other in the name of religion and race. I was desperately shocked to see piles of dead bodies and to be affronted by the smell of death. (I was to be faced with such horrors again in Sri Lanka, where it also seemed to me that similar fanaticism was to blame.) The Jewish people that I had met in England had always been extraordinarily civilised, yet here were Jews with hatred in their eyes and murder in their hearts.

I remember that I felt no fear, only a great calmness. It is extraordinary how fear departs when one is surrounded by horror. I was told only recently by President Jayawardene of the extraordinary calm he felt during the assassination attempt on his life in the Sri Lankan Parliament. Of his colleagues sitting round the President's table, two were instantly killed.

I have always been intrigued by other cultures and their people. After my first visit to Jordan, I became interested in the history of the Arab people and the ancient races who had lived around the shores of the Mediterranean.

The logical thing to do was to go and spend a certain amount of time in an encampment among the Bedouin. I learned the merest smattering of Arabic, and it became crystal clear that a common language was of the utmost importance. I cannot pretend to have shared an intellectual relationship with those I met, but there was a good deal of non-verbal communication and I discovered that under these mysterious robes and veils were some extremely beautiful women. Around the camp fire, I ate succulent and highly spiced lamb and encountered sophisticated and philosophical men.

Of course it would have been ridiculous to have done all this without first reading the books of T. E. Lawrence, and I came increasingly to understand the fascination which the timelessness of the desert and the nature of the Arab people held for him and for numerous other Englishmen.

What the Bedouin made of me I cannot possibly tell, but I would imagine they got considerable pleasure out of watching me attempting, disastrously, to master the art of camel-riding.

It could hardly have been in greater contrast to the time I spent on a kibbutz in Gallilee. Here, there was no problem of communication. The dusky maidens were replaced by beautiful girls with blue eyes and fair hair.

The desert became the lush environment of primitive but successful farming, where interesting ideas about crop rotation were being developed. It was all entirely self-contained. Everything was shared. Everything was discussed. I was free to express my strongly held views about the Palestinians and to try to justify them. But to my mind, the religious observances were in contradiction to the professed Marxism of the kibbutz lifestyle. A Utopian concept, but something had been sacrificed – the family life without which no community is complete.

As a result of these experiences, I became involved with an organisation called the Council for the Advancement of Arab/British Understanding, and I was the Chairman of the East Anglian branch for ten years. The purpose of this organisation was to balance the propaganda emanating from the Israelis, who – of course – had total mastery of the business of public relations. If a solution was ever to be found to the continuing tragedy of the Middle East, and the violence contained, it was essential that both sides of the argument were clearly and fairly understood by the world community. There was certainly no possibility of a meeting of minds between the Islamic fundamentalists on the one hand and the ultra-orthodox Jews on the other.

Nobody could have an interest in the Middle East, or experience anything of the Middle East, without being aware of the remarkable General Sir John Glubb, usually known as

Glubb Pasha; his influence as a soldier in the development of the Kingdom of Jordan, his gentle but warrior-like qualities, his dismissal by Hussein, and his continuing work to spread the message of Anglo-Arab understanding throughout the world. He was a soldier, but he was also a philosopher. What he had experienced as a soldier had greatly influenced his philosophy. Furthermore he had the rare gift – both in his written works and in his spoken words – of absolute clarity.

He was one of the first international speakers whom I invited to address the English-Speaking Union when I became chairman of the Norwich branch. Naturally, he attracted an enormous crowd and was able to field questions from those who were hostile to him – as well as those who hero-worshipped him – with aplomb. He spoke passionately about the symbolic importance of the English language. To him, the language and the culture it represented were one. Afterwards, we drank a bottle of whisky together and discussed philosophy late into the night. He was a tiny man with thick, white hair and a pronounced twinkle in his eye; he was also a great man, with that necessary adjunct to greatness, an incurable optimism.

His memorial service in Westminster Abbey was dramatically heralded by a huge thunder-clap. It was very moving towards the end of the service when King Hussein got up spontaneously to pay tribute to the little soldier whom he had thrown out in the early and troubled stages of his remarkable reign.

Further travels took me to most of the countries of Europe, and I felt the language barriers most acutely. English, of a sort, was spoken by many in the Middle East and throughout most Commonwealth countries. I found it strange that those with whom the British shared an older cultural heritage were divided by the formidable chasm of language.

I was thirty when I ran out of money. I remember flagging down a taxi, only to discover that all I could pay the driver with was a bottle of champagne. Obviously travel had to come to at least a temporary halt.

About this time I met my future wife, Jennie Lubbock. We had been introduced by one of Norwich's most gregarious and endearing characters, Anthony Gurney, and after a couple of years we married. Naturally enough, she was curious to know not just how, but where we were going to set up house. I was living in a large and heavily mortgaged place in Norwich surrounded by antiques – many of which had to be sold to keep me going. This house too was sold and we moved temporarily into my wife's cottage just outside Norwich.

It was at this time that I met by chance Paul Bradshaw, a financial and investment adviser. Under the misapprehension that I was very wealthy, he set about his sales pitch. I was impressed with his grasp of financial planning, and since I was looking for a major source of income, asked him if he thought I could have a career in money management. He told me that my talents would be particularly suited to the promotional side of the business.

"There are a lot of people like you," he told me, "who really don't understand the need for financial planning. You probably look after yourself pretty well, but when it comes to money, you leave everything rather to luck." I admitted that that was absolutely true.

He then showed me how to read the Financial Times for profit, not merely for interest. He taught me that currencies, for instance, are at least as important as market movements. I also realised that my natural interest in current affairs and politics and the knowledge which I had acquired from my experiences abroad could have a huge bearing on financial matters.

It was not long before Paul Bradshaw and I were in partnership as Bradshaw and Wynne-Parker and attracted considerable funds from people who realised that their finances were not being adequately managed by bank managers or building societies.

Things were different in the City in those days. There was still an atmosphere of good trustworthy amateurs, and a deal could be sealed with a gentleman's handshake. There was less bureaucracy, greater freedom for the entrepreneur, and – in short – under the restrictions of the recently-introduced Financial Services Act, I do not believe that Paul and I could begin to do today what we did then.

The essence of the service we provided was to take over the handling of the client's investment portfolio and insurance affairs with a fee system, which I had come across in America, based on profit. If we didn't make a profit, we didn't get paid. Such an incentive helps to concentrate the mind admirably!

After some two years, Paul and I parted company amicably and I continued with my own business, Wynne-Parker Financial Management, which was to attract several million pounds of investment over the next few years. This financial management business was later to diversify into a variety of other business interests, now known as the Wynne-Parker Group.

In the early days though, I discovered the importance of investment diversification. Real estate in America was one profitable area, after which I became interested in the diamond markets in Tel Aviv, Antwerp and London. In any young business, mistakes are inevitable – and this was my big one. The diamond market tumbled. I lost so much money that I thought I was going under. However, I did somehow manage to cling on, and it was fortunate that I did, because eventually the price of diamonds recovered all its traditional strength.

Diamonds led me to sapphires. Blue, which is the colour of healing, has always been a favourite colour of mine, and the blue in sapphires ('sapphire' is the Greek for blue) I found especially attractive. The richness of a good ruby is irresistible, and the cool green of the emerald a great pleasure, but for me the sapphire is nonpareil. There is considerable misunderstanding about the distinction between the ruby and the sapphire. The truth is that there is no clear demarcation, since both are gem varieties of corundum. But modern practice is to call corundums of all colours except red sapphires. The red ones, of course, are rubies. Both are next in hardness only to diamonds.

The cutting and polishing of diamonds and sapphires to investment standard requires considerable skill. The famous Cullinan diamond, as large as a human fist, was 'cleaved' by the firm of Asscher in Amsterdam in 1908. From that massive diamond, nine large and 96 smaller brilliants were cut.

Caratage is of prime importance. Once again, it may be useful to correct a common misapprehension. To the goldsmith, the carat is a designation of quality, whereas to the gemologist it is a designation of weight. Since 1907, the metric carat has been adopted worldwide, each carat relating to 200 mg. And although the value of a precious stone is proportional to its weight, the proportion is not a simple one, since the larger a stone the rarer and more precious it is considered to be. Nor is size the only criterion. Colour is vital, while other qualities like lustrousness and transparency are also regarded. Few of these quality sapphires are set as jewellery; the majority are classified and then secured in strong-boxes and bank vaults. The finest examples are, and have always been, excellent investments; a rule which applies to the finest examples of just about everything.

The sapphire is the national stone of Sri Lanka and it was in Sri Lanka that the largest known sapphire, a stone weighing 42 lbs, was found. Buddhists love the blue of the sapphire, but for many Muslims it is an unlucky colour, and the chances of selling sapphires in certain parts of Asia are remote.

As I say, it was diamonds which led me to sapphires, and it

was sapphires which led me to Sri Lanka for my first visit, in 1981. There are fine sapphires to be found in Burma, Thailand and parts of South America, but it is my belief that the blue Sri Lankan sapphire is superior to them all.

The success of my business made it not just desirable but necessary that we should find somewhere more permanent to live and bring up a family. We were fortunate to find Saxlingham Lodge, a pleasant Georgian house a few miles south of Norwich, and have lived there ever since.

I enjoy field sports. Norfolk is primarily shooting country with hunting a close second. I am also a keen beagler. However the sport I find most engaging and challenging is stalking, which, for me, is confined to the highlands of Scotland and enjoys a relatively short season. With a half-dozen friends there is really nothing more pleasant than to stalk by day, and have stimulating conversation round a candle-lit dinner table by night. To my way of thinking, stalking is not just the least cruel of all field sports – the stag is unaware that he is being stalked until he is shot – but the most romantic, with a fine literature.

Incidentally, there is an uncanny similarity between the Scottish highlands and the hill country of Sri Lanka where Sir Samuel Baker hunted elk with his famous hounds.

I have always been a keen party-giver (at my most impoverished, I remember throwing an extravagant champagne party), and in Norfolk I had built up an interesting circle of friends and acquaintances and led a busy social life – in contrast to the exhausting hard work involved in developing a business.

Despite the socialising and the business, it was still a surprise when I was telephoned by an acquaintance called Dudley Layton and asked whether I was prepared to take on the chairmanship of the Norfolk branch of the English-Speaking Union. I was wholly ignorant of the organisation and I am not proud to recall that my first question was how much of my time the chairmanship would take. Just a few meetings a year, Mr. Layton told me. Little did I know!

Within a few days I found myself at the A.G.M., in the process of being elected Chairman. So swift was my elevation that I found myself in the chair before I had officially joined the organisation. Whether or not this is unique, it is clearly a most unhealthy precedent. I was just twenty-nine, though looking perhaps a little older, and flattered to be the youngest branch chairman of the English-Speaking Union.

Membership was some 200. There was a woman doctor with great personality and firm opinions, a university lecturer or two, a few local businessmen, and a splendid group of dedicated ladies. I think I grasped almost at once that they – and I – belonged to an organisation with immense potential. At the local level our ambitions may have seemed modest; the traditional social functions and fund-raising activities, the occasional visiting speaker. But this was the grass roots, and being associated with it was hugely valuable to me. Today I am one of the few governors of the ESU who has been a branch chairman, and I find when I visit other branches in the U.K., in America, in India, Pakistan or Sri Lanka that the grass roots are much the same wherever you travel.

My rise in the ESU was rapid indeed. Within a year of becoming Branch Chairman I received a telephone call from Major General William Odling, the then Chairman of the East Region, inviting Jennie and myself to Sunday luncheon. During lunch, Bill asked me whether I would consider taking over from him as Regional Chairman, "to bring youth and dynamism to the job". Never being one to reject a challenge, I agreed with alacrity and at the next Annual General Meeting of the East Region found myself elected chairman – the youngest Regional Chairman ever!

I followed in the line of three illustrious predecessors. First

Sir Stuart Mallinson, stalwart East Anglian, powerful personality and Founder Chairman whom I only had the privilege of meeting a few times in my early months as Norfolk ESU chairman. Next James Abinger, Essex neighbour, who has never failed to offer me very sound advice – I usually follow it – on ESU affairs, and who had also been my proposer for the Carlton Club. Then came Bill Odling who had brought all the organisational skills of a good soldier with him to produce the most efficient region in the ESU.

And now it was my turn.

My subsequent election to the ESU National Council for England and Wales, and later my Governorship of the ESU of the Commonwealth, might not have happened if Bill had not proposed me as Regional Chairman. And who knows whether the rest of this story could have been written without that sequence of events?

The most important consequence of my experience as a Branch and Regional Chairman was, as I say, my involvement in the grass roots of the membership. I realised at once – and have never forgotten – that the ordinary members are the heart of any organisation; especially so in the ESU with its stress on 'people-to-people' diplomacy.

Despite being Regional Chairman, I continued as Chairman of the Norwich and Norfolk branch for five years. Within the first year, I had the pleasure of welcoming the Sri Lankan High Commissioner, and enjoyed his vivid descriptions of life in Sri Lanka. Little did I know how closely linked my destiny was to become with that beautiful but tragic island.

However, it is high time I gave a chapter or two to a history of the English-Speaking Union, which means effectively the history of one man, Sir Evelyn Wrench.

Chapter 3

THE FOUNDER

"What Others Have Dreamed He Has Done"

Inscription in the courtyard of Dartmouth House

I
Schoolboy

To understand the English-Speaking Union, it is essential to understand the unique personality of its founder, Sir Evelyn Wrench. It was not until I recently discovered and read his two published autobiographies that I did so. And not just his personality, but also the curious coincidences and circumstances which prompted him to abandon a career which would have taken him to the very top in newspaper publishing for an ideal; an ideal which even today is still some way from fulfilment.

Evelyn Wrench was born in County Fermanagh in 1882. His father, an Englishman, was an Irish Land Commissioner, and the family were Orange through and through. As a boy of five, his favourite reading was the catalogues of the Army and Navy Stores, in which could be found colourful illustrations of the paraphernalia of imperialism, tents and tropical helmets, high-stepping horses and uniforms, clocks and cameras and canoes.

An early desire to become an engine-driver was subverted into a plan to amalgamate all the railways in the British Isles under the title: "The Great British and Irish Railway Company", with a first class runaround ticket over the entire system to be available at £8–10–0. Already, the boy showed signs of the business skills which were to be such a feature of his early career.

In 1893, young Evelyn was sent to board at Summer Fields, an exclusive and academic prep school near Oxford. He survived his first term well enough by giving his best postage stamp 'swaps' to the largest and most aggressive of his potential tormentors.

One of his earliest trips abroad was a family outing to Holland. Just ten hours after leaving Harwich, the boat docked at Antwerp next to a cargo steamer flying the red ensign. Evelyn's mother and sister were amused to hear him exclaim: "How wonderful it is to see the British flag again!"

He was a delicate child, catching every infection that he was exposed to, and once, when there was none, alarming his family by swallowing a penny. For thirteen days all were on tenterhooks; the boy studied books on anatomy, the doctor insisted on a diet of potatoes, porridge and spinach, until, wonder of wonders, the penny re-emerged. Evelyn became a local celebrity, and the penny secured an honoured place in the cabinet of family curios. A more serious bout of influenza led to inflammation of the lungs and a small bottle of champagne each day was prescribed.

In 1896, Evelyn was sent to C. H. Allcock's house at Eton, where he was supremely happy, keeping dormice, joining the beagles, and reading Walter Scott. But it was the School Corps which gave him the greatest thrill. After the celebration of the Jubilee in 1897, with a military-style procession, Evelyn concluded that: "We are the people of destiny. It is evidently our job to run the world."

It was Evelyn's mother who was the most energetic in encouraging foreign travel. During the summer of 1898, a holiday was planned to take in Asia Minor and the remoter parts of Europe, and it was Evelyn, then 15 years old, and his sister who were entrusted with the planning of the tour, the negotiations with Thomas Cook's, and the handling of the money. In Germany and Holland he was impressed that he saw no slums, no beggars. In Russia he was flattered to be followed everywhere by the secret police, and he enjoyed his first Russian food (some

39 different dishes at a single sitting) and his first vodka.

In his Russian diary he records the news of Kitchener's historic victory at Omdurman: "Our killed and wounded numbered 500, while the Dervishes lost 15,000 killed and 16,000 prisoners."

During his last year at Eton, he debated the issue: "Whether Anarchists should be allowed freedom in the Queen's Realms". He concluded that they should, because "it was in the interest of their cause to see what a Queen Great Britain has got, and even if they do not like her, they cannot help respecting her, since after all, they are human beings."

More and more passionate grew his interest in matters imperial. He mourned over those territories which were no longer coloured red on the map: Morocco, Dutch East Indies, Corfu, Heligoland, parts of South America, and, most tragic of all, the United States. He prayed nightly for the Empire to be extended "wider still and wider". Indeed, he could see no real reason why the whole world should not be ruled by Queen Victoria.

He had moments of doubt. When he visited the Eton Mission in Hackney Wick and saw the human pigsties there, the conditions alarmed and troubled him, but not for long.

He was alarmed and troubled for a great deal longer by the guilty anxieties of adolescence, and, one can guess, reading between the lines, that Wrench's puberty was a difficult one. But his conclusions are characteristically enlightened. In 'Uphill', his first autobiography, published in 1934, he writes: "(No boy) should be threatened with the disgrace of expulsion from school. If his elders could once win his confidence and let him feel that he was not alone in his struggles, that they were going to stand by him whatever happened, a great advance would be made. . . Fear will never eradicate vice, but love might."

Evelyn left Eton two years early. His ill health was exacerbated by the notorious Thames Valley dampness, and his longing to travel more widely persuaded his parents to take him away. But first there were a few months at home in Ireland.

He visited a Missionary Exhibition in Dublin and was much affected by it. He decided that instead of being British Ambassador in Paris, his erstwhile ambition, he would become a missionary, but this decision was as short-lived as the previous one. Instead, he worked part-time in his father's office at the Irish Land Commission, and studied at Trinity College with a private tutor in the afternoons.

A second trip to Russia was even more influential than the first. He was hugely moved, as I was to be later, by the rituals of the Eastern Orthodox Church: "I forgot my neighbours and looked up beyond the clouds of incense to the golden reredos. Wonderfully robed priests and their assistants in the dim distance moved methodically about. Men's voices chanted in old Slavonic in a deep bass – of course I could not understand – but perhaps I did understand. The language they were using required no words, it was the eternal language of the Soul."

And yet, and yet, back in Ireland had he not been taught that in the Roman faith lay all the machinations of the Anti-Christ?

Then again, the boy had believed it was only a matter of time before the whole world came under British rule. However, now he had seen a small part of the Russian Empire, he had to revise his imperial ambitions. The Russian Empire extended to eight million square miles. You could fit Canada, Australia, South Africa, New Zealand, Newfoundland and Britain into it, and there would still be room to spare. And this territory was contiguous, and was host to an ancient civilisation, a culture, a religion which owed nothing to the West. What was worse it seemed neither to know anything about the Queen – few Russians had even heard of her, and even fewer knew that she was about to celebrate her Diamond Jubilee – nor to care at all.

One thing was clear; the bear was not about to be swallowed up by the lion, so both would have to learn to live in peace.

From Russia, the party moved to the Caucasus, the Crimea, and Asia Minor, where the Wrench family fed the stray dogs of Stamboul, stood amazed by the whirling of the Dervishes, travelled by the German-built Baghdad Railway, and returned by boat via Athens and Marseilles.

It was a sad homecoming. The Boer War was going disastrously wrong and there were many in Dublin who scarcely troubled to hide their delight. For Evelyn, such treacherous displays were almost more than he could bear.

II
Postcard King

At the age of 17, Evelyn was sent to a German family to become fluent in the language. For eight happy months he stayed in a 16th Century castle in Weilburg and was the only Englishman in a community of three thousand Germans. Despite the kindness of his host, the local agent for the Grand Duke of Nassau, and his host's family, he continued to be troubled by the news from South Africa, and the desperate conditions of the besieged garrisons at Ladysmith, Kimberley and Mafeking. Naturally, the Germans took the side of the Dutch Boers, and one evening, when the six-year-old grand-daughter of the house was sitting on Evelyn's knee, looking at the photographs of the war in a newspaper, she exclaimed: "Die bosen Englander und die armen Boeren" (the wicked Englishman and the poor Boers). It was not long before Evelyn had taught her to switch the adjectives around.

In 1900, Germany was in the grip of postcard mania, and the young Englishman was intrigued to learn from the local innkeeper that on a busy Sunday he could expect to sell as many as 250 postcards. Evelyn, always a keen philatelist, was intrigued. During eight months in Germany he would have sent maybe 200 cards to his family and friends. If every German sent as many cards in a year, then the total annual output must run to – well, the mathematics were staggering; perhaps 4,000,000,000. The German cards were excellently produced, unlike in England where the now familiar, full-sized, oblong postcards had only recently been made legal. If an enterprising young man were to expand the German postcard market to England, was there any reason why he should not make a fortune for himself?

On holiday with his mother and his sister near Dresden he shared his enthusiasm. One should select only the finest artists and photographers. Why not introduce into England those revolving display stands on which the cards looked so attractive to potential customers? Why not . . .? Charlotte, Evelyn's mother, fired by her son's energetic speculations, sent a telegram to her husband:

> *"Evelyn sees business opening wish you would join us to advise wire reply Charlotte."*

The reply by return was encouraging:

> *"Shall be with you Wednesday or before."*

With his family solidly behind the enterprise the 17-year-old entrepreneur returned to London to research the market. He visited likely tourist sites. He inquired about photographers and printing processes. He took premises in the Haymarket above a tailor's shop, and procured official business cards. He registered a trade-mark: a wrench, naturally. A bank account was opened at Coutts, the overdraft manager being a keen amateur photographer who was intrigued by the nature of the business. And then the Old Etonian network was brought into operation. Lord Esher at the Office of Works gave permission for the Wrench series to be sold at Hampton Court, Holyrood House, Carisbrooke Castle and elsewhere within his purview. Old General Millman at the Tower of London was eager to be of use. The only problems arose with the German printers. Everything was ready, salesmen and retailers were on hand, but there was nothing to sell. The young man's frustrated energy and his business instincts combined to produce a fever of impatience, not uncommon among businessmen, until at last the first consignment arrived.

The early weeks of entrepreneurship were unglamorous. There was endless leg-work. There was the need to be humble and self-effacing with some shop-keepers, confident and self-assured with others. The Old Etonian network could no longer be put to use, but perhaps the experience of having been a fag was valuable.

There were coups. Captain Scott agreed to help with the plan for a series of twelve postcards with lithographed autographs by each of the members of the *Discovery* expedition. There were *faux pas*. The final card in the series depicted a polar bear but, as almost every school child knows, there are no polar bears at the South Pole. Nonetheless business flourished. Seven months after opening his office, Evelyn was writing home: "182,000 cards arrived from Germany on Friday and 75,000 on Saturday. We did £250 worth of business last month."

By November 1902, sales were up to £1,950 in the month. Within three years of its inception the enterprise had moved to premises in New Oxford Street where one house proving inadequate, a further three were added and walls knocked down so that the four intercommunicated. In 1903, Evelyn was voted a salary of £500 by the Board and the staff had grown to 60, with a dozen salesmen round the country. Evelyn sailed to Germany and placed orders for five million postcards. The Wrench Series Catalogue was 64 pages long.

But those triumphant years for Evelyn were tragic for the family. His brother died. His father lost his fortune in South Africa. His mother had a serious tumble from her bicycle and was to remain a semi-invalid for the rest of her life. Evelyn's health, never robust, was weakened by overwork, and there were times when he worried about what he referred to as "my starved soul". But work was the best analgesic and he worked ever harder. He enlarged his ambitions. A postcard empire was all very well, but there was more to be made out of life than that. He studied the career of Joseph Chamberlain who had grown rich out of manufacturing screws and had moved on to become Prime Minister.

He was encouraged to dream such dreams by the amount of press attention which now centred on him in America, where he became known as the "souvenir postcard king", as well as at home. At a banquet for his twenty-first birthday, guests included newspaper proprietors. It seemed that the sky was the limit. Until you looked closely at the sky and observed the thunderclouds massing on the horizon.

Evelyn was not looking at the sky, he was looking at postcards. He devised a scheme of loaning postcard stands to retailers, who were not required to pay for them; they were not even required to use them exclusively for the Wrench series of cards. But the stands did ensure that the postcards were handsomely displayed. Unfortunately seven or eight thousand pounds of hard-earned capital was locked up in those beastly stands. The value of them should perhaps have been written off in the books. It was not. And perhaps it had been too generous to have paid the sales manager a commission on turnover, where most companies paid commission on net profits.

Then there was the self-imposed requirement to keep a stock of over 10,000 cards, while constantly adding new series until the target had been reached; a Wrench Series for every town and tourist resort in the country. More capital locked away in unloved and unwanted and often unsaleable stock.

Three months after his banquet, the postcard king went cap in hand to the Amalgamated Press for capital. Amalgamated Press put in £8,000 in the form of a debenture. But financial problems took the fun out of the business, and Evelyn went to stay with Alfred Harmsworth, then editor of the Daily Mirror, on the French Riviera. In the Rooms at Monte Carlo the young tycoon discovered the delights of roulette. It was a simple matter. You put your ten francs on zero, and when zero came up you walked away with 360 francs. Or maybe you left the 360 francs on zero and walked away with 12,960 francs. Or maybe your luck changed and you walked away with nothing. Evelyn's did and Evelyn did.

In any case, money had lost its seriousness for him. Amalgamated Press was running the postcard business now. Let them get on with it. Evelyn bought a seven-horse-power Panhard with borrowed money, hired a chauffeur, toured Ireland and showed off the beautiful new toy to the disapproving old family.

It was better to be out of London, for in London, it was decided to put the business into liquidation. A Receiver was appointed. Two years later the Wrench postcard empire was no more.

It had been a painful experience, but a valuable education. The young man had grown up. He had had to roll up his sleeves and do business with representatives and retailers, printers and packers. He had learned the mystique of figures, and how they can be made to dance by clever accountants, and how they do not always mean what they seem to mean. He had learned that no matter how often you count them, chickens do not always hatch.

III
Newspaper Man

In July 1904, Evelyn Wrench was invited to lunch at de Keyser's Hotel by Lord Northcliffe, who offered him a job as his confidential secretary. In November, he took on additionally the duties of sub-editor of the new overseas edition of the Daily Mail, where he worked with a dreamy young man called Edgar Wallace. Promotion continued to be rapid. Within a year he had become assistant news editor, and then for four months the editor of the Weekly Despatch. (The joke current in Carmelite House was that a dinner should be given to ex-editors of the Weekly Despatch "only no dining-room in Fleet Street was large enough".) In the winter of 1905, he was appointed editor of The World with instructions to "buck it up". And in 1906, Northcliffe granted him two months leave of absence to visit Canada and the United States.

In Canada, where "the romance of Empire took hold of me", Evelyn's first engagement was with Sir Wilfred Laurier, the French-Canadian Premier of the Dominion. Sir Wilfred shocked him to the core by advocating a union of all the nations of the Anglo-Saxon world. A union that excluded the United States? Perish the thought! It is at this point in his autobiography that the future direction of Evelyn's career becomes inevitable.

"In future always at the back of my mind," he writes, "was the haunting knowledge of this dual problem. How were we to organise the far-flung sections of the British Empire to greatest mutual advantage and, at the same time, how best to promote understanding between the two sections of the English-speaking race? It is curious that I largely owe to a Frenchman the conception of English-speaking unity – a cause for which I have worked ever since."

On board the train, the 'Imperial Limited', and roused by a meeting with Lord Grey, the Governor-General, a keen proponent of the British Empire, Evelyn wrote a long document in which he set out his vision of a Commonwealth of Free States.

He was aware of the many organisations which already existed; the Royal Colonial Institute, the Victoria League, the Daughters of the Empire, the Empire League, the Empire Day Movement, the Navy League, the British-Made Goods League, and dozens of others, and he recognized that what was really needed was one grand umbrella organisation, with a target membership of a million souls, and 15 clearly defined aims, and concluded: "A poor and unknown man has built the Salvation Army to its present position in some thirty years. With influence, the power of the press behind us, and money, verily we can attain even greater results." The only unclear thing in the document is who the "we" might be.

He returned to Fleet Street and six busy years during which his star as a newspaper man continued in the ascendancy. His memories of his weeks in North America were happy ones, but his plans for an Empire Society remained in his mind, germinating, awaiting the moment half a dozen years hence when they could begin to become real.

In May 1907, Lord Rothermere appointed him Manager of the Export Department of Associated Newspapers and the Amalgamated Press, and sent him for two months to manage the Paris Daily Mail. He went racing at Longchamps and Auteuil, where he found himself excited by seeing fashionable women wearing the creations which he had previously seen worn by the mannequins in the perfumed trying-on rooms of the Rue de la Paix. He shopped at Le Printemps and Les Galeries Lafayettes, and dined at Les Ambassadeurs in the Champs Elysees or La Tour d'Argent or Au Vrai Robinson, a restaurant built in a tree-house, each course being pulled up in a specially constructed basket. He watched Sarah Bernhardt act and La Belle Otero dance, and chased the blue bird of happiness in distracting feminine company. Despite which, Lord Northcliffe seems to have been delighted with what Evelyn achieved.

Indeed, his capacity for hard work continued undiminished. Back in London he records that he had worked in the office for 30 days without a break. This was overdoing it and once again his health suffered. He was sent away to the sunshine, which meant Tunis with his father and to Spain for a three-week holiday with Lord and Lady Northcliffe.

He travelled ahead of the Chief and Lady Northcliffe to prepare everything against their arrival. On the journey to Seville the train ran over a huge bull and was derailed.

The Spanish house belonged to the British Consul and had a large marble patio "open to the sky, and with a garden of roses in full bloom clustering up the walls". There was a large and colourful staff and a carriage had been hired which came complete with coachman and footman wearing yellow cockades. Evelyn was impressed.

But his gentle susceptibilities were appalled by the savageries of the bull-fight. "I can't understand why the Church permits it," he wrote. His love of ritual took him to an Easter Procession, although his description of the impressive scene has sinister undertones as we read it today:

"The most interesting procession was at 2 a.m. during the night between Good Friday and Easter Sunday. The whole

Square of San Lorenzo was in darkness, suddenly the doors of the Church were thrown open and thousands of lighted candles became visible. A procession of five hundred black, purple or white figures emerged carrying candles. The figures were enveloped in cloaks from head to foot. Over their heads they wore peaked hoods like sugar loafs. There were two slits for the eyes. The dress dates from the Inquisition."

Not that it could have been much of a holiday. There was Northcliffe's correspondence, the daily news reports to type out, the household to be kept running smoothly. One day the two men went for a long walk at Alcalar. It was here that Evelyn confided his plans for an Overseas League to promote the British Commonwealth, and Northcliffe promised him the freedom of the columns of the Overseas Daily Mail to advertise the idea.

An interesting colleague at this time and later was Norman Angell, whom Northcliffe had appointed to head the Continental Daily Mail in Paris. Evelyn discussed with him his plans to start "a great Imperial non-party brotherhood". Angell believed in world unity. He published a book called 'The Great Illusion' in which he argued the futility of war; you could not even expect to make a profit by winning any longer. The book was not just an enormous best-seller with sales of over a million; it was hugely influential. Unfortunately its message was not taken to heart.

Travelling to Ottawa on behalf of the Amalgamated Press, Evelyn arrived in a heat-wave. His malarial symptoms returned. He became lethargic and feverish with a temperature of 104. Typhoid was diagnosed. For a week he hovered between life and death.

During two months of recuperation in Toronto he thought seriously about the pattern of his life. Was the world any better for his existence? Why was he so absorbed in the ephemeral? Northcliffe had said that good health was all in life, but what was the point of being alive and well if you did nothing useful with your life? Northcliffe paid for Evelyn and his sister, who had been nursing him, to take a cruise to the West Indies. In those days the islands were not much visited by the British and Evelyn was stunned by what he found:

"As we sailed the Spanish Main I stepped back into the world of Charles Kingsley's 'Westward Ho!' I was again caught up in the glamour of the Elizabethans. What fun Sir Francis Drake, Frobisher and Hawkins must have had "singeing the King of Spain's beard", and plundering the treasure trove of His Catholic Majesty. . . Modern Empire-building seems tame in comparison.

"In the late afternoon the mountains of Jamaica hove into sight. There was a wonderful sunset, a purple sea and a sky of crimson, orange and salmon. This is my first experience of a British tropical colony. I cannot describe the wave of elation and emotion that swept over me. I had dreamt of this moment. The balmy air, the smell of cinnamon, nutmeg and strange spices, the dark faces on the badly lit quay, all combined to make me feel as in a dream. These strange beings were my fellow subjects. How wonderful to be a British citizen."

Worshipping in the church he was happy to record that there was no colour bar, and he thanked God for Wilberforce.

He returned to the office, renewed and refreshed, on the first day of 1909. The doorkeeper was friendly. There were fresh flowers in the room. He made resolutions in his diary: to become a more efficient human being; to concentrate his energy on the big things but to develop *every* side of his nature. This last resolution stemmed apparently from a conversation with a woman friend who accused him of calculating everything to further his career, and told him pointedly that what he really required was "to be head over heels in love". Ironically his career continued to flourish without, it seems, his calculating it.

On 12th January, he was delighted to be appointed sales manager of Amalgamated Press, a big step up with a healthy salary of £2,000 a year. His promotion came at a meeting with both Northcliffe and Rothermere. The added responsibilities gave him an energy and a pleasure in his work which recalled the heady days of the postcard empire.

For three years he toured the industrial cities and towns of Britain and exposed to the slums and the squalour, he lost his political complacency. A typical diary entry records: "Passed 200 unemployed on my way home, shuffling along the Embankment on their way to a soup kitchen. The cost of my dinner would have fed the lot. Think of it."

At the end of 1909, Evelyn paid his third visit to the United States, visiting San Francisco just three years after the devastating earthquake, but, as he records, an entirely new city had arisen on the rubble of the old one.

He was overwhelmed by his first sight of the Grand Canyon, describing it with characteristic energy, and concluding that after the Grand Canyon everything else seemed tame.

And in New York he had long conversations about the woeful history of Anglo-American discord with Dr. Walter Hines Page, who five years later was to be appointed U.S. Ambassador to the Court of St. James. Page was to be hugely significant in the ESU movement. It was an historic meeting of minds.

IV
The Overseas Club.

King Edward died on 6th May 1910. Evelyn watched the funeral in great comfort from the Marlborough Club. In the afternoon he attended the Memorial Service in Westminster Abbey, where funeral marches by Beethoven, Tchaikovsky, Mendelssohn, Purcell and Chopin were played. To a man as easily swayed by ritual as Evelyn, the experience was overwhelming. "I was shaken to the foundations of my being," he recorded. "I was linked up with all who had suffered." His ambitions to make a great career in newspapers "withered like a plucked windflower". His days with Northcliffe were numbered.

His reading habits changed. Now we find him reading such improving essays as Bosanquet's 'Poor Law Report', J. S. Mills's 'On Liberty' and Cotterill's 'Human Justice for Those at the Bottom'. He gave up smoking and alcohol. He continued to play golf, but developed an irritating slice, which is disastrous at Royal Sandwich. He visited prisons, interested himself in the Borstal Movement and concerned himself with the Hollingden Boys Club in Clerkenwell.

More pertinently he showed Northcliffe an article he had written describing his proposals to form an Overseas Club, and Northcliffe, lying at full length on a dark red leather sofa with his back to the light to protect his eyes and puffing at cheap German cigars, gave permission for its publication in the Overseas Daily Mail.

The Club was to be "an organisation to draw together in the bond of comradeship the peoples now living under the folds of the British flag". It was to be "strictly non-party, non-sectarian and open to any British subject". Aflame with enthusiasm for his project, Evelyn rashly added that there was to be no annual subscription.

Within a fortnight, the Club had 160 members, by the end of the year 12,000. For a shilling badges were provided with a strikingly symbolic design and the overpage inscription:

THE CREED OF AN IMPERIALIST

I believe in our glorious Empire of Free Peoples,
In the sacredness of our mission,
In the unselfishness of our aims.
I believe in our great past
And in a greater future,
In the emptiness of riches
And the dignity of labour.
I believe in right thinking and pure living
And in the inspirational power of woman.
I believe in national re-birth,
In a new Empire and a new world.
I believe in the need for humbleness,
In the vision of the mountain tops.
I believe in God's guidance in the days ahead.
I believe.

Those who desired more specific directions as to just what it was Evelyn had in mind were told that the Overseas Club was "a kind of grown-up Boy Scouts".

Unfortunately for Evelyn, there are many people in the world who would do anything to avoid helping old ladies across the street and those who are altogether too cynical for the Boy Scouts. Word got around that the Overseas Club, for all its grandiose pretensions, was in effect nothing more than a circulation stunt. Indeed that was probably the view of Lord Northcliffe himself. Patriotic as the Daily Mail and its proprietor might be, Evelyn was quite unable to persuade himself that the welfare of the country and the welfare of the Daily Mail were indivisible.

Thus a rift grew up between the newspaper magnate and the brilliant young man (Evelyn was still only 29) in whom he had invested so many of his hopes. To Evelyn, Northcliffe had become an enigma. How could such an accomplished man dedicate himself to so much that was essentially trivial? No doubt to Northcliffe Evelyn had also become an enigma. How could a young man with one of the most envied positions and incomes in Fleet Street be prepared to throw everything away for an ideal, and an ideal with no annual subscription at that?

The London season of 1911 was one of the most glittering ever. Evelyn was appointed Gold Stick Officer for the Coronation Service. At the Shakespeare Ball he went in the costume – a Venetian red cloak – of Proteus from 'The Two Gentlemen of Verona'. He lunched with, among others, two particularly promising young men, Winston Churchill, who was to become a chairman of the English-Speaking Union, and the future Lord Beaverbrook. But all the time he was being tugged in different directions; Lord Northcliffe offered him a directorship of Amalgamated Press, while Sir Harold, later Lord Harmsworth, gave him six months leave of absence to pursue his visionary ideas on a tour of the Empire.

On 27th June, Evelyn played host to the first international meeting of the Overseas Club, later to become the Overseas League. Present were some 300 members, who were visiting London for the Coronation. A "high note of Imperial fervour pervaded the audience" and the speech – over which Evelyn had taken particular trouble – was a great success. It was a splendid omen for the speeches he was going to have to make in less favourable places and in front of less sympathetic audiences on his tour.

The Daily Mail behaved generously, believing perhaps that Evelyn's enthusiasm might burn itself out if given its head, and that in any case he was likely to prove a useful ambassador for the newspaper to which he owed so much. Sir Harold agreed that he should receive a sinecure of £1,000 a year for three years in the capacity of Manager of the Export Department. He had been eight years with Northcliffe, and Northcliffe was reluctant to let him go. Why not put "a man" in charge of the Overseas Club and continue with his career? As a rich and successful magnate would he not carry more clout when it came to advancing the cause of his new baby? These were powerful arguments, and Evelyn was tempted.

But it was his dream, and nobody else could dream it. In May 1912, he set off on what he called, with a fair measure of accuracy, his Empire Crusade.

He began in Canada, where during the course of a ten week tour he addressed 35 public meetings. There were banquets, public lectures and open-air meetings. At an important Empire Day meeting in Ottawa, Evelyn was thrown when an elderly gentleman sitting opposite him fell asleep as he began to unfold his vision of Empire. In Alberta he stood on a chair in the garden of the chairman of the local group, while thunder growled and lightning flashed on all sides and four large white pomeranians romped and barked. A more serious distraction was a cable from Northcliffe demanding to know why he had not received credit in Evelyn's public pronouncements. Evelyn realised yet again that the help he had received from the Daily Mail carried with it a weighty responsibility.

Wherever he travelled he found time to read. In Canada, Carlyle and Ruskin were the strongest influences. Ruskin had supplanted Cecil Rhodes' place in Evelyn's heart, and he no longer accepted imperialism without a strong admixture of social conscience. "So long as there is a slum in the cities of the Old World," he wrote, "so long as there is corruption in public life in the Empire, patriots must hang their heads in shame."

From North America he returned to Britain for two months rest, setting off again in October to Australasia via Italy, the Suez Canal and the South Sea Islands. What exactly was he after? "A kind of grown-up Boy Scouts" dedicated to Empire

Service was how he came to define it.

The New Zealand visit began with a fiasco. He almost tripped as he came ashore along the gangway, and on that first night he dreamed that a badger was springing at his throat. The organisation was a shambles, and the work of planning the tour had to begin again from scratch. Only the beauty of the islands and the support of his sister, who had become an accomplished public speaker and able to take much of the pressure off him, sustained him during these difficult days. He found New Zealand a contented country and could identify no evidence of prejudice against the Maoris. A Maori minister referred in a speech to the gradual absorption of his race by the British: "In the past it was we who 'absorbed' you. Now you have turned the tables on us." Evelyn reports that this "joke" was widely taken up by the press. One wonders if the minister had really been joking.

The high spot of the whole tour came at the end, with a visit to Robert Louis Stevenson's tomb in Vailima on what is now Western Samoa. The memorial is reached after a demanding and sweaty climb through the forest. A hundred native Samoans had dragged Tusitala's coffin up that mountainside in 1894, but there were compensations at the top. Flaming red hibiscus guarded the tomb, whence one had a spectacular view over the Pacific. Where the teller of tales lies is a sarcophagus, on the side of which is carved the lines:

"Under the wide and starry sky
Dig the grave and let me lie.
Glad did I live and gladly die,
And I laid me down with a will.
This be the verse you grave for me,
Here he lies where he longed to be;
Home is the sailor, home from the sea,
And the hunter home from the hill."

In Australia, Evelyn suffered for three weeks from deep depression. How could he expect to influence anyone, how ensure that any enthusiasm he was able to generate did not dissipate as soon as he left for the next venue? Why had he not stayed in London and enjoyed the fruits of his remarkable successes? But the tour gathered momentum. The politicians seemed surprisingly sympathetic. At Brisbane on Empire Day 1813, there was an audience of more than 2,000, and at Perth for the farewell meeting of the tour, 2,400. The Governor attended, as well as the Boy Scouts, and a silver band fired those present with patriotic fervour.

Evelyn arrived in South Africa with the cast of a touring production of 'Kismet', which travelled complete with Nubian slaves, donkeys and a snake. It had taken them seven hours to find a hotel that would accommodate them in Sydney. One wonders how on earth they managed in Durban.

Everywhere in South Africa Evelyn was confronted with racial and political issues. There were South African Dutch and European Dutch (Hollanders) and Voortrekkers; there were Zulus and Kaffirs and Indians. Everybody told Evelyn that South Africa was "a black man's country" and likely to remain so. The Dutch were dead set against introducing British immigrants, and it is a credit to Evelyn's skill as a public speaker that on more than one occasion he was able to enrol into the Overseas Club Dutchmen who had fought against the British in the War.

But it seems that while Evelyn was able to deal with the Dutch, he was flummoxed by the continuing mischief-making of Northcliffe. Those who had signed up as members of the Overseas Club were immediately circularised with invitations to become subscribers to the Overseas Mail. In the circumstances it became more and more difficult for Evelyn to persuade editors of rival newspapers that the tour was not just a publicity campaign on the grand scale.

In Cape Town, Evelyn was taken to Rhodes park and Groote Schuur (Great Barn), Rhodes' home. In Muizenberg he visited the little thatched cottage in which Rhodes died with the words: "So little done, so much to do" on his lips.

The tour covered 64,000 miles, the equivalent of three circuits of the globe. Evelyn Wrench gave 250 public speeches. "In future", he wrote, "I always saw Great Britain through Dominion eyes." He concluded that "old-fashioned doctrines of white predominance must go by the board. Equal rights for every civilised man is the only logical goal. We must take all these nations into partnership when they are ready for political advancement."

Back in Carmelite House he was given the smallest office he had ever occupied, even in his postcard days. His stock was at zero. But he had an important job to do, which was to raise enough money to open a London centre for the Overseas Club. It did not take long. On 24th May 1914 – Empire Day – the Lord Mayor of London opened the premises at General Buildings, Aldwych, and Evelyn moved his membership files out of Carmelite House.

What others had dreamed he was now ready to do. How he did it will be the subject of a later chapter.

Chapter 4

THE LAND OF DREAMS

"And oh my soul remembers
When you have sailed the seas away
And the English climate's chilly
And the English skies are grey,
You will see with a sudden vision
You will see with a sudden sigh
The scarlet clad flamboyant
Awash the azure sky."

W.S. Senior.

I was maybe seven years old, a bored little boy in a school classroom. It said Geography on the timetable, and the subject with which we were to deal was Ceylon. The talk was of an island smaller than our own, an island of palm trees and elephants and paddy fields. I knew little and remembered less of its history. I could not have marked its position on the map. But that night I had a dream. I was in a paddy field. It was wet and humid. The landscape around me was very green and the paddy fields were surrounded by thick undergrowth and tall trees. There was a smell of rich earth which was hot under my sandalled feet. I felt at home, as though this was where I belonged.

Once, in Jerusalem, I had met the Bishop of the Nicobar and Andaman Islands and the conversation had turned to Ceylon (as it then still was). I was reminded of that boy, that classroom, that dream. Much later when I had become the chairman of the Norfolk and Norwich branch of the English-Speaking Union, the Sri Lankan High Commissioner, Mr. V. Mendis, came to address us and spoke of his country. He had neither film nor slides, and he spoke rather fanatically – it seems to me in retrospect – about Independence. However, halfway through his lecture I recalled that young boy and that geography lesson and that dream of palm trees and elephants and paddy fields. It is not often that a Sri Lankan High Commissioner comes to Norfolk. It was my good fortune to be there when he came.

Was it just coincidence that a few years later my business interests were to require me at last to visit the island which was so very different to our own? Or was it true, as Albert Schweitzer had once said, that there is a significance in events?

Sri Lanka is pearl-shaped, and has come to be known as the Pearl of the Indian Ocean. One of its early names was Ratnadvipa, which means island of gems, and its inhabitants believe (and have always believed) that the gems in which their island is so rich have magic properties. For instance, the Navaratna ring contains nine varieties of precious stones and is believed to bring peace and contentment to its owner. And the Gomedaya is a garnet, which some believe will protect the wearer against evil planetary influences – although the stones need to be flawless and in contact with the skin if the protection is to be powerful. When I first visited the pearl island, I was quite convinced that if I put my hand into the river bed, I would certainly pull out sapphires and rubies in plenty.

Clearly, when I became interested in the investment possibilities of sapphires Sri Lanka would have to be visited. C. J. R. Whittle, a business friend, had already started importing sapphires from Sri Lanka and he was one of my companions on my first trip to my dream island in 1981.

The Air Lanka flight comes in to land at Colombo at about six in the morning. If you've been awake in a window seat you will already have seen the arid plains of South India. Then you see the mist, and through the mist what appears to be the deepest of jungles. The impression is of greenness, powerful, lush greenness. As you descend details become clearer, coconut groves and a cluster of tiny islands shimmer into focus. Sri Lanka at last!

My one formal invitation was from N.U. Jayawardena – familiarly known throughout the island as 'N.U.' partly to distinguish him from J.R. Jayawardene, the ex-President – and the telephone number of a certain Dr. T. P. Amerasinghe.

'N.U.' has been called the Paul Getty of Sri Lanka. It is no exaggeration to say that he literally walked out of the jungle bare-footed to school, where he studied to such effect that he was to become the first indigenous Governor of the Bank of Ceylon. He has been described as a workaholic; certainly, he is a multi-millionaire, an economist, a philosopher – and a friend. It was he who generously took me under his wing and showed me the operation of the mining industry; from the traditional ceremony at the start of the work when the Sinhalese miners light an oil lamp and place it inside a cage of coconut leaves, through the excavation of the "illam" (gravel) and the washing and sorting of the stones, to the cutting, polishing, examination and certification of any gems suitable for setting or investment. (An official certificate may double the value of your stone. Once certified it is placed in a polythene sachet and sealed with a microfilm attesting to its quality and ownership.)

On my fifth night on the island I was invited to dinner by 'N.U.' It was a great privilege, since he gives the most lavish and splendid dinner parties imaginable. We were 20 or 30 guests who sat down to dinner under the tropical sky and the stars which seem in that part of Asia to twinkle with extraordinary brightness. Waited on by impeccably turned-out servants, we drank delectable wines and ate the most delicious Eastern delicacies while the conversation flowed.

It was over the extraordinarily good port (I made a note of it in my diary but, alas, it has vanished) that he spoke to me of Sri Lanka's emergent economy, and notably of Lanka Carbons, a company – now public – which manufactures activated high grade carbons out of coconut husks and exports them to mining concerns all over the world. Soon afterwards I became a director of that company, and it provided me with a major area of investment activity. A high risk venture, as things turned out, with numerous management and technical problems. The ten rupee shares dropped to four rupees but eventually were trading securely at 40, by which time the company was usefully employing Tamil, Sinhalese and Muslims. Successful businessmen always believe that business is not an end in itself. It can become socially, intellectually and even philosophically satisfying; certainly I found it so in the case of Lanka Carbons.

I am writing now of a period when Sri Lanka was energetically looking for trading links with other countries. J.R. Jayewardene had taken his oaths of office as Prime Minister and first Executive President in 1977 and instituted a series of economic measures which were of huge significance. Quotas, import restrictions and subsidies were swept away. Three massive development schemes, involving the diverting of the Mahaweli River, the establishment of an Investment Promotion Zone at Katunayake and the building of tourist hotels and facilities, were instituted. Within five years bank deposits rose by 298%, minimum wages by 145% and the cost of living by 105%. I sometimes wonder how much richer and more stable Sri Lanka might be today if 'J.R' had succeeded Dudley Sennanayake as Prime Minister in 1953.

During my first week in Sri Lanka I had not a moment to myself. But during the second week I remembered I had an introduction to Dr. T. P. Amerasinghe. All I knew about him was that a friend in London, Alan Lee Williams, former Labour M.P. and Director General of the English-Speaking Union, had called him "perceptive" and had insisted that we would get on extremely well. After several false attempts – in 1979 the Sri Lankan telephone service was not something to boast about – I reached him and introduced myself.

"Thank you for ringing," he said, "but of course we have met before." I denied this, explaining that I was on my first visit to the Island. We arranged to meet at the swimming pool of the Inter-Continental, where I was approached by a man small in stature but with a firm and friendly handshake.

"You were on the plane from London," he said, "and you kept me awake the whole journey because I couldn't help eavesdropping on your conversation."

We laughed about this and enjoyed a drink together, when it soon became apparent that our meeting was remarkably opportune. He told me that he had been a barrister, a schoolmaster, a politician in his youth. The conversation turned inevitably to the ESU, and my chairmanship of the Eastern Counties branch in England. Why, I wondered, was there no branch in Sri Lanka? It seemed ideal. The good doctor had touched on the fact that English was about to become the third national language after Sinhalese and Tamil, and that the President was something of an Anglophile, admiring not just the language, but the legal, constitutional and parliamentary systems as well.

Traditionally on the island, English had been the language of the educated classes who, some said, had treacherously abandoned their linguistic birthright. And the English that was – and is – spoken there was precise and pure, what you might call BBC Radio Three English. But then in 1958 the Sinhala Only Act was introduced and for a generation after Independence the ethnic languages were promoted at the expense of English, which was not even taught in the schools. To my mind this policy was wholly misguided. Tamil and Sinhalese became hostile languages to the Sinhalese and the Tamils respectively; as a neutral language English was available to both. It is, of course, important to remain loyal to one's roots, but one is also a citizen of the world and one needs to live in the world and trade with the world. Clearly therefore, one should also be able to *speak* to the world.

Not all of this emerged in our meeting at the Inter-Continental swimming pool, but we both acknowledged our mutual respect for the English language and all it represented. It is no exaggeration to say that within half an hour we were determined that a Sri Lankan branch of the English-Speaking Union should be set up, and that within a week its foundations were laid.

Dr. Amerasinghe's energy was exemplary. He knew that the first priority was to get the right people on your side, and in next to no time he had secured the patronage of President J. R. Jayewardene. Others almost as distinguished followed: a leading politician, then headmistress of a girls' school, a university professor, the High Commissioners of Britain, New Zealand, Australia, Canada and India.

I realise now, and perhaps I realised then, just how fortunate I had been to meet the good doctor. I have come to learn in business that the success of any new venture depends almost entirely upon the selection of the right personnel. Put the right man or woman at the helm, and progress is assured. Dr. Amerasinghe was not just the right man; it sometimes seemed to me that he was the *only* man!

I do not know how old he is, and I have never felt inclined to ask him. He appears to me to combine the wisdom of many years with the sparkle of eternal youth. He is at ease with all ages, all castes and all classes. He is as much at home in the chambers of a London barrister as he is lighting incense in a buddhist temple in Sri Lanka. As a young man he joined the Socialist Party and fought for independence. But politically he has come full circle and now has a healthy regard for the present President Premadasa. Having learnt English first from his mother and later from missionaries he was unique in his ability – quite early in his career – to write speeches in English for aspiring politicians and to teach them how to deliver those same speeches, for he is as much a master of the spoken as he is of the written word. On a purely practical level it was his remarkable contacts which ensured that our ESU work in Sri Lanka would grow and prosper.

We sent a telegram to the International Council of the ESU

based at Dartmouth House in London, applying for membership, although we knew that our application would have to await recognition until the next full meeting of the council.

An important priority was the little matter of premises. For the first few weeks we made do with my hotel suite and our secretariat consisted solely of Amanda Good, working with me on the gemological front. Together we set out our initial plans which, besides the acquisition of premises, consisted of the setting up of both an English language newspaper to promote the ESU, and English classes open to everyone.

Eventually I had to return to England. But within a few months of my departure we had been enabled to rent our original headquarters in Sir James Pieris Mawata, Colombo. The H.Q. was to include what has very graciously been called the Wynne-Parker Library, to which I and my fellow East Anglians have contributed some 4,000 volumes. It included a small administrative office and also offered primitive accommodation for our first English Language classes.

It had been a fruitful three weeks. I had gone to Sri Lanka with the intention of discovering as much as I could about the mining and production of sapphires; I returned having made friendly contact with the then President J.R. Jawardene – our first ESU Patron in that country – plus Dr. Amerasinghe. With their co-operation, I had set up the Sri Lankan branch of the ESU.

Back in London there was more ESU work to be done. For one thing I had to rally support for the new branch from the British section and from the International Council members. Membership is by no means automatic. Bophuthatswana's application was turned down on racist grounds. (The argument, which I did not support, was that Bophuthatswana was too much under the sway of South Africa; my own view was – and is – that evolution is taking place in South Africa as it is everywhere, and that we have to help it along howsoever we can).

Then there was the not insignificant matter of funding. Due to financial restrictions, the ESU has never yet been able officially to fund any new Commonwealth branch, and it was crystal clear that the enthusiasm of the very dedicated people in Sri Lanka could not be immediately matched by hard cash.

So I went back to my East Anglian ESU Region lobbying round the branches and setting up a formal structure, known as the East Regional Sri Lanka Educational Fund. This had double benefits. It raised money, of course. But it also enlarged the horizons of the ESU members in the region, to catch their imagination, to encourage them to consider the world beyond their own experience. A distant country which you have never visited and which you have no plans to visit can seem very unreal.

I further determined that part of the money raised should be used to bring over to England young Sri Lankans, so that our generous supporters could see the results of their generosity.

Within six months of the establishment of the ESU Sri Lanka, we were able to bring over to the 1982 English-Speaking Union's Summer School at Jesus College, Oxford, two students – Ruwan Fonseka, and Mrs. Krishni Jayawardene. Both have developed an interest in the ESU and now serve on the Sri Lankan ESU Appeal Committee; in fact, Ruwan is now our Treasurer. We selected them, and others since, for their intelligence, their ability to communicate well in English and their interest in the world at large.

Fortunately the weather for the Summer School was uncharacteristically wonderful. The theme was "Britain Today", and speakers included Sir Monty Finniston on British industry, A.L.Rowse on historical Oxford, Baroness Young on foreign policy, Robert Lacey on the Monarchy and Sir Peter Newsam on race relations. Other subjects dealt with were Britain in

Europe, Britain and the Third World, broadcasting, the Parliamentary system, women in the eighties, trades unions, Northern Ireland, and the Commonwealth today.

The students enjoyed a cruise on the Thames, a visit to Stratford for a production of 'Julius Caesar', a concert in Holywell Music Room (the oldest music room in Europe), a garden party at Rhodes House and parties and dinners almost every evening.

A visiting American from Nashville recorded her impressions: "As marvellous as the lectures and planned events were, I can't honestly say they were my fondest memories of my trip to Oxford. In reflecting upon my time there, the one thing that pervades my thoughts is the leisure time spent with newly-made friends. How well we all mixed, how open we were with one another, how easily we established close friendships; the memories of these feelings will not fade or change, even if the friendships themselves must over time and distance."

Another 13 students have attended the Oxford Summer School from Sri Lanka since that first occasion and they were always given hospitality by ESU Members. When these students returned home for a career in industry, the arts or politics, they did so appreciating the strength and friendship of the international organisation to which they belonged, while the English people with whom they stayed could see the benefits brought by their generosity. It would be splendid if we could institute a reciprocal scheme for British students to visit Sri Lanka; to date all we have managed is to welcome two young girls from Norfolk, one of whom worked at classifying the library books, while the other taught in the school.

The first English classes we held in Sri Lanka were for Buddhist monks. They were inaugurated by the then Minister of Justice, the Hon. Dr. Nissanka Wijeyeratne, who became one of our staunchest early supporters and remained so. He was at pains to insist that the monks needed to learn English not only so that they could spread their message to a wider world, but also so that they could assimilate and absorb the cultures of other communities beyond their own. A two-way traffic.

The Buddhist clergy are a power to be reckoned with on the island, and there is a clear parallel to be drawn between the influence of the Buddhist clergy in Sri Lanka at the present time and the influence of Catholic monks in mediaeval England. These early classes of 1983/4 were extremely well attended and the rows of splendid aesthetic faces of saffron-robed monks, almost indistinguishable to the teacher, were something of an inspiration to us all. About three years ago, I attended the dedication of a Buddhist temple by the Prime Minister and I was introduced to the Chief Priest of the village. One of his assistant monks came up to me and, producing a certificate from his pocket, said: "Oh yes, Mr. Wynne-Parker, I learned English at the ESU School."

From these classes more than a hundred Buddhist monks have graduated, along with 300 other students.

Ever since they were set up, it was decided that ESU classes must be offered free of charge to the poorer people – and at the most basic level they were. The most anybody pays is the odd rupee. We have estimated that it costs us about £25 a head to educate a child, starting from scratch and taking him or her up to a useful conversational level.

But besides these free classes we went to the opposite extreme on Saturday mornings, with classes for bank managers and the leaders of industry in the commercial area of Colombo. These were for businessmen who had a smattering of English but needed to perfect their business skills. They were expected to pay a reasonable fee to help subsidise our other classes and they were given courses calculated to teach them a practical basic English in 90 hours.

Also on Saturday mornings classes were held for mentally handicapped children. This, I had particularly encouraged, as my friendship with Brian Rix had led to my becoming a Governor of the MENCAP City Foundation.

When there were criticisms of our English classes, they tended ironically to be criticisms of technique: why have the English become so lazy in the way they use their language? Dr. Amerasinghe himself won a prize in a poetry competition after displaying his ability to quote any poem by heart, from the very earliest poems extant to the late romantics.

Recently we have given top priority to our classes for young children from the ages of five to thirteen. The peripheral classes continue of course, but the children's classes are paramount – and the demand is enormous.

In February 1988, I had invited Group Captain David Hicks, the Deputy General of the ESU, on his first visit to Sri Lanka, to the inauguration of a new series of English classes based on the Callan Method – a technique which places the emphasis on the spoken rather than the written language.

The traditional lamp was lit, symbolising the blessing of the Buddha on the work; work which on this occasion marked an important conjunction of the religious and the secular. There was a sea of young faces eager to learn, but none of them understood a single word of English and the only way to communicate with them was through written notes. Some would have travelled 40 miles yet, however poor, the little girls all wore immaculate white dresses and the little boys sported pressed white shorts. The temperature must have been more than a hundred degrees Fahrenheit and – despite the comforts of a large fan – we were absolutely exhausted by the end of the half-hour ceremony. But the classes began just as soon as the ceremony was over.

Some four months later, James Spain, the American Ambassador, a fervent supporter of the work of the ESU, came to present prizes at the annual prize-giving. It was reported to me that two of the children, a boy and a girl whom we had seen at the inauguration of the classes in February, addressed the audience for some minutes in extremely confident English – no small achievement in such a short time. At the time of writing (July 1989) over 500 youngsters are attending our courses with equally impressive results.

The ESU of Sri Lanka is growing apace, with influence far beyond its relatively small membership of less than 1,000. Since 1981, most of the funding has come from the UK; naturally the pound sterling can achieve far more than the rupee. Our first premises in Sir James Pieris Mawata were found and rented courtesy of Mr. A. Hathy Sulaiman, a man large in personality as in stature, and one of the Muslim minority. These we have quickly outgrown, as the English classes attract enormous support; one advertisement alone receiving 1,200 applications for space which was stretched to accommodate 100!

The Wynne-Parker Library was opened on 10th February 1987 by Dr. Nissanka Wijeyeratne, then Minister of Justice. It contains more than 4,000 volumes with an interesting specialist section on tropical diseases. There are encyclopaedias, dictionaries, works on the English language, and a wide diversity of literature. It has been – and will remain – a free library for the people of the island.

We must never forget just how valuable a book can be to an average family in a village in Sri Lanka. On my first visit, my driver, William Fonseka, took me to his little house in the jungle; corrugated roof, bare bricks. Apart from a bed and a heavy mallet used for bashing cobras on the head whenever they dared to slide under the door, there appeared to be only two possessions of any significance. One was the television set. This was most impressive and was covered by a protective sheet. The other was a book. I resolved then and there to get into Sri Lanka as many books as I possibly could. I further decided that central to our ESU work there must be an adequate library freely available to all who wished to use it. It would have to be a reference library; the quickest way of getting rid of books, of course, is to open a lending library. So we collected books in Norfolk and other parts of East Anglia and I added some volumes from my own library, until we had a selection to be proud of.

I remember being asked to find a set of the Encyclopaedia Britannica and was delighted to uncover in a Norwich bookshop the last series to be published in Britain. I had the books packed up and taken to the Post Office, but was horrified to learn how much it would cost to send them, even by second class mail. Fortunately the Ranfurly Library came to our assistance and have since freighted books out for us at just £100 per consignment.

The Wynne-Parker Library, important as it undoubtedly is, is by no means the only ESU venture of importance. Perhaps of equal significance is our newspaper, Open Mind. The first edition, specially bound in green leather, was presented to President Jayewardene at a ceremony at the President's house on 20th February 1984. On the front page were the following lines which I wrote for the newspaper and quoted to the President:

"We are both island peoples.
Both live within the shadow of a great continent.
Both have an ancient history of civilisation.
Both are influenced by great religions.
Both enjoy freedom of speech.
Both remain broadly independent.

Both have tremendous opportunities for influencing the course of history."

The President responded by saying that all island peoples felt a great affinity. He said he had been greatly moved by Mrs. Thatcher's courageous response to the plight of the Falkland Islanders and reminded me that he had been the first Third World leader to congratulate the British Prime Minister. It would be nice, he added wistfully and a touch prophetically, to think that the British could aid us similarly if attacked by India. (The Indians did indeed invade Sri Lankan waters, but in the event, and despite a great international outcry, there was little that the British could do.)

Dr. Amerasinghe was the perfect choice for the editor of Open Mind. His knowledge of Asian literature in general and Sinhalese literature in particular is remarkable. Moreover, his love for English literature and his ability to quote from it extensively must be unique. The title Open Mind was fortuitously chosen.

The traditional ESU Commonwealth magazine was called Concord, presumably based on Concord House, the headquarters of the organisation in Wrench's day. Then about ten years ago, some very bright person came up with the idea that we ought to change our image; and part of the image-change was to replace the title Concord with Open Mind. The old guard amongst the membership was horrified and within a year the new title was rejected in favour of the original Concord.

So with the title Open Mind unwanted and unloved, Dr. Amerasinghe and I decided to steal it for our Sri Lankan magazine. This has flourished, and some feel that it compares favourably with Concord. Not in its appearance and lay-out, perhaps, for its presses are basic and it costs a modest 4 rupees (those who cannot afford even this get it free), but its literary standards and the standard of many of the incisive and provocative articles is extremely high. It is produced quarterly and, besides literature and politics, it covers news ranging from cricket, to the ESU. Soon we hope to be able to publish it monthly, and to turn it into a significant fund-raiser.

But the library and the magazine are only a part of our ESU programme. Besides those students sent to the ESU summer schools at Oxford, a further five have gone to the Callan School of English in London and one to the London Berlitz School. Public debates are held on the English language in the context of the Sri Lankan ethnic problem. Seminars and literary luncheons are held. One of my dreams is that the ESU in Sri Lanka might get together a compilation of some of the greatest works in Sinhalese literature – it is an especially rich literature going back many centuries – translate them into English and publish them. But this dream remains secondary to the vital work of educating the local people in the English language.

As the ESU of Sri Lanka developed its activities, support for it was growing not only in the East Region, but in London. This support had started at the ESU of Sri Lanka inaugural dinner held at Dartmouth House on 3rd June 1982, which was presided over by Sir Patrick Dean – then Chairman of the ESU of the Commonwealth. Dr. Amerasinghe was guest of honour and other speakers included the Sri Lankan High Commissioner and Miss Adele Abharatna.

What was not reported in the press was that at this dinner Mr. Desmond de Silva QC., a fellow member of the Carlton Club, met Princess Katarina of Yugoslavia, the daughter of my old friend, Prince Tomislav. They married five years later at London's Serbian Cathedral and a reception attended by many members of the Yugoslav, Sri Lankan and British communities followed. The Wynne-Parker family led a large ESU contingent to wish Mr. de Silva and Sri Lanka's latest princess many happy years.

Ever since this inaugural dinner, support for the Sri Lanka ESU has grown; it has been encouraged by occasional visits to Dartmouth House of leading Sri Lankan figures, including Nissanka Wijeyeratne and High Commissioner Chandra Monerawela.

As I have written, our first headquarters in Sir James Peiris Mawata was rented and was becoming far too small to accommodate our developing activities. Its ambitions were far-reaching, but its income was modest. Having gained considerable confidence with the success of the Dartmouth House Appeal (described in a later chapter), I decided it was essential to launch an English-Speaking Union of Sri Lanka Appeal. Our aim would be to raise enough money to purchase a suitable headquarters and to build up a capital base.

The Appeal was launched at the Oberoi Hotel in Colombo on 30th January 1989, at a ceremony presided over by the legendary Dr. M.C.M. Kaleel, President of the United National Party. Messages of support were received not just from the former President J.R. Jayawardene, a friend of the Sri Lanka ESU from its earliest days, but from the dynamic new President, Ranasinghe Premadasa, who has given us every encouragement to expand our work.

A word or two about this remarkable man, Ranasinghe Premadasa, eighth Prime Minister of the Democratic Socialist Republic of Sri Lanka. Born in the heart of Colombo in 1924, he was educated at home by doting parents until he was seven, when he was sent to the temple school where he quickly acquired a knowledge for the Buddhist texts and a love for the lore and doctrines of Buddhism. From the temple school he transferred to a girls' school, the Harward School in Pettah, and then to Lorenz College, where classes were in English and where young nationalists and freedom fighters argued late into the night. His formal education ended at St. Joseph's College, where he earned a place in the football team. Buddhism, sexual enlightenment, nationalism and Catholicism all featured in young Ranasinghe's upbringing – a heady mix!

His social conscience was alert to the squalour and illiteracy that he observed on all sides and while still in his teens, he started a Sunday School and a night school at which he tried to instill a modicum of literacy into those students brave enough (for the school was greeted with some hostility) to come along.

With the support – both moral and financial – of his father, Premadasa entered politics in 1950, when he contested a seat for the Colombo Municipal Council. He won, and devoted his time to improving the housing in the slums of Kehelwatte and opening the Mihindu Maha Vidyalaya School. Within five years he was Deputy Mayor, and within six, under the influence of the late Prime Minister, Dudley Senanayake, he had joined the UNP.

In 1964, he married Hema Wickrematunge, a devoted Buddhist, a social worker, a political campaigner and a patron of the arts. The Premadasas have two children. From 1965, he sat in Parliament for the constituency of Colombo Central, and cabinet posts followed quickly. But housing was still his principal concern, and the Maligawatte Housing Scheme was his triumph. Seventy-five acres of marshland were turned into attractive homes.

From 1970–77, the UNP was out of office, but when Jayewardene's government was finally returned to power in an overwhelming landslide of votes, Premadasa became Prime Minister. Retaining his housing portfolio, he built 153,000 houses in five years and opened up 200 new villages.

His interests include the theatre, photography, sport and writing novels, two of which have been filmed. He gets up at 4.30 every morning, and works till late. His philosophy is perhaps best summed up in a speech he made in Hawaii in October 1980: "If I am asked what is the 'ism' that the new Sri

Lanka government professes, if there is a desire to have a name for it, I can say it is pragmatism. We meet a situation, we find solutions. We do not have ready-made solutions for incoming problems. When we face a problem we find a solution to it and this is the sort of vision and philosophy we are trying to generate in the minds of our people in Sri Lanka. This strength has to be developed."

No sooner had our Appeal for almost ten million rupees (about £170,000) been launched, than it was decided to purchase our new headquarters in Colombo. Prices were historically low as a result of the troubles, and I felt that if we delayed, such a splendid opportunity for premises in the very centre of the city would never recur. A loan was negotiated with the Hatton National Bank through the good offices of Lester Cooray, the Chairman, who died at the tragically early age of 52, just two days after my arrival for the Appeal Fund launch.

The decision seemed quickly to be justified, as I received immediate pledges of support. Nimal Cooke, of the Maharaja Group, promised £10,000 and Dr. Marcus Barccani-Dunston, who had generously supported the U.K. Appeal (described in Chapter Six), pledged £7,000. Help and advice was offered and accepted by many, especially in Colombo, by Anton Wijeyegoonewardene, to whom I was introduced by Asitha Perera, and in London by both Sir John Nicholas, now Chairman of the Friends of Sri Lanka Appeal and by my friend Frank Noah.

It is our intention that the new centre will also house a college for the training of teachers. It scarcely makes economic sense to bring over teachers from Britain when already in Sri Lanka there are plenty of highly intelligent English-speakers – many of them the young retired who would like nothing better than to undertake this valuable work.

The financial problems we have faced in Sri Lanka have been considerable. We started in a very humble capacity and failed to capture the imagination of the fashionable Colombo set. In London, Dartmouth House is in the elite centre of Mayfair and is considered very much the fashionable place to be and to be seen. Not so in Colombo, where only recently has the significance of the work we are doing become generally known.

Colombo is a metropolis of a million cosmopolitan people. It is a port, a commercial and banking centre, a city in which rickshaws still mingle with Mercedes and life continues at a hectic pace. The social life is an energetic one, and includes many fashionable dinner parties. Television is not watched to the same extent as it is in Britain, and the rich do not experience a servant problem – so parties can be thrown at very short notice without moans or groans from the wife.

In recent years, there has been a relaxation of the caste system, enabling a more interesting cross-section of guests to meet at evening functions, and an enthusiastic but ignorant foreigner such as myself has been able to get away with organising larger and more democratic parties than have been traditional on the island.

Not so very long ago, dinner parties would have been for men only, and it is not uncommon today to see the ladies, particularly the older ones, in a huddle at one end of the room. And this in a country where women gained the vote just three years after they did in Britain. These days in Colombo, the hostess presides over the dinner party just as prominently as her husband. Invitations will specify dinner at eight o'clock, but if you arrive at eight you will probably find your hostess still in the bath. You sit down to dinner between nine and ten and stay seated until the early hours. Conversation ranges widely over political, cultural and international matters.

It would be a serious mistake for the ESU in Sri Lanka to underestimate the importance of such occasions in broadening its base and helping to raise funds for its English classes. I see nothing cynical in such a policy. The ESU stands for traditional cultures, but it supports the ideal of communication at every level, and practises and preaches tolerance above all else.

It is said that travel broadens the mind. I believe this saying to be true. My own experiences in Sri Lanka have caused me to reflect – and my reflections have led me to conclude – that an individual must be true to his or her heritage while recognising the validity of others.

Two great heresies have bedevilled political and religious thought for far too long. They are the heresies of Utopianism and ecumenism. Both heresies were born out of a worthy desire for unity. But both are dangerously unrealistic. Let us recognize that traditions have evolved through the God-given and natural inclinations of individual groups. Rather than seek for an unattainable World Government or World Religion, let all who differ agree to differ and gain through their differences mutual enrichment and respect.

Personally I have found no conflict between an inherited appreciation of my own cultural traditions (Western, democratic, monarchist, Anglican) and the respect I share with the ESU for my friends who are Eastern, Buddhist, Hindu or Moslem, and republican. On the one hand I sense that all these varieties of human existence are of no ultimate significance; on the other I recognize how humans crave an identity and consider them therefore to be of enormous immediate importance.

A healthy co-existence which encourages all to recognise and respect the differences of others while doing everything possible to improve the means of communication is, I believe, not only desirable but achievable. But I acknowledge, too, that we have no right to force change on others nor to assume that they will in the end come round to one's own point of view. Why should they?

Little did Dr. Amerasinghe and I know how far-reaching would be the consequences of our meeting on the aeroplane.

Chapter 5

THE ISLAND OF SPICES AND THE SACRED TOOTH

"Devo Vassatu Kalena
Sassa Sampatti Hetu Cha
Phito Bhavatu Loko Cha
Raja Bhavatu Dhammiko."

"May the rain fall in time
May the harvest be rich
May the world be prosperous
May the rulers be righteous"

Traditional

According to archaeologists, *homo sapiens* existed on Sri Lanka half a million years ago. There is clear evidence of Mesolithic man living in caves about ten thousand years before Christ, warming his hands at a fire, but eating his food raw and possibly eating his friends. Later cultures lived in the dry zones (the northern and south-eastern plains), settling around the river banks, living on rice.

For the early history of Sri Lanka, one has to turn to the Mahavamsa, a Chronicle written, so the scholars say, in the 6th Century A.D. (Professor Kingsley de Silva argues for the 5th), and its sequel, the Culavamsa. According to these works, the island was first colonised in the 5th Century B.C. by Vijaya, and his 700 rowdy companions, who had been expelled for misconduct from the Kingdom of Sihapura in Northern India. It is an intriguing story and the truth is probably that Sri Lanka was settled by Indo-Aryans from just this region.

To return to the Mahavamsa, it appears that Vijaya invited his younger brother to join him as his successor, but that the brother sent his son, Panduvasudeva, instead. Panduvasudeva landed at Trincomalee with an entourage of 32 companions, and was enthroned at Upatissagama. The story suggests that the early settlers were followed by a second group of colonising Indians, which is exactly what you would expect. The author (or authors) of the Mahavamsa used the chronicles to show that the founding of Sri Lanka was simultaneous with the passing away of the Buddha in Northern India. The Buddha, the Guide of the World, is recorded as having commended Vijaya and his men to the protection of the God Indra and promised on his death-bed that where they landed would become the place where the Buddhist religion would be established and prevail uncorrupted down the ages: "In Lanka, O Lord of Gods, will my religion be established".

It is vital to appreciate that the Sinhalese see themselves as the ultimate guardians of the Buddhist faith, the chosen people; and that for them race, religion and national identity are inseparable.

Certainly we know that a Buddhist Mission was sent to Sri Lanka in the time of the ruler Devanampiya Tissa, who was converted, and that the spread of the religion was speedy, assimilating those cults and rituals and exorcist ceremonials that already existed on the island. During the second half of the 3rd Century B.C. the Theri Sanghamitta brought from the land ruled over by her father, the Emperor Asoka, a branch of the actual bo-tree (Ficus Religiosa), under which Buddha had attained enlightenment. It took root and still survives on the island at Anuradhapura, the oldest recorded tree in the history of the world. Sadly the original bo-tree on the mainland was destroyed centuries ago by a fanatic.

During Dutugemunu's reign (161–137 B.C.), Buddhist temples were built throughout the island with impressive dagobas such as the Ruwanveli and the marvellous Brazen Palace, Loha Mas Pasada.

According to Fa Hsein, a Chinese visitor to Sri Lanka in the 5th Century A.D., the island contained no human inhabitants, merely "spirits and *nagas* with whom merchants of various countries carried on a trade". Whether they were spirits or rather more substantial, the inhabitants traded most successfully. Two hundred years later Hsuan-Tsang referred to Sri Lanka, after a failed attempt to visit it, as: "Lanka, the holy land, centre of the Theravada . . . without a knowledge of whose books none can know Buddhism".

Besides the Brahman Aryan settlers from Northern India and the Buddhist missionaries from the Mauryan Empire, there was another group of early settlers, the Dravidians, a race of Tamil merchants from Southern India. Thus early in its chequered history a multi-ethnic society was established on the island. From Vijaya's arrival to Sri Vickrama Rajasimha in the 19th Century, some 295 kings reigned over all or part of the island.

Sri Lanka was unique for its remarkably sophisticated irrigation system. The waters that flowed down from the mountains were channelled into reservoirs and canals which exhibited an impressive knowledge of trigonometry and hydraulic principles. The Kantalai tank built by King Mahasena (274–302 A.D.) covered 4,560 acres, was fed by a 25-mile canal and contained within a 50-foot high tank. The Kalawewa of King Dhatusena covered seven square miles with a dam three-and-a-half miles long and up to 58 foot high. A 54-mile canal, known as the Yoda Ela (Giants Canal) linked it to the city of Anuradhapura. The first 17 miles had a gradient of a mere six inches a mile. An equally impressive reservoir, the Parakrama Samudra, was built in the 12th Century by Parakramabahu I, a most influential King; nothing like it was to be attempted again until Sri Lankan independence in 1948.

The total system of dams, canals, sluices, locks, weirs and underground conduits was unsurpassed in antiquity, and has never been equalled in the modern world for its sophistication and elegance.

The irrigation system led to a flourishing agricultural economy and great wealth. Anuradhapura, the northern cultural centre, became a remarkable monument to Buddha with magnificent *stupas* (solid hemispheric domes). The largest of these, Jetavanarama, is taller than St. Paul's Cathedral and nearly as tall as St. Peter's in Rome. With palaces, parks, reservoirs and statues, it was one of the greatest cities of the world, rivalled in Sri Lanka only by Polonnaruwa in the east.

Ancient Sri Lanka was feudal. The dynastic kings had absolute autonomy but the nobles, the merchants and the monasteries were encouraged to become powerful land-owners. There was a caste system but in Sri Lanka this had no basis in religion and was less rigorous than in India.

From time to time, adventurers from South India would be tempted by reports of the immense riches on the island and attempt to seize power. Increasingly, Sinhalese rulers would hire Tamil mercenaries from India to help them settle local differences. Only once did the whole island fall under Indian rule, and that was for seventy-five years in the 10th and 11th Centuries under the Cholas, from South India, when the capital of the island was shifted from Anuradhapura to Polonnaruwa. Here they felt safer with their backs to the friendly north, and the Mahaveli protecting them from surprise attacks from the south.

But in 1070 A.D., the Cholas surrendered to the indigenous armies under Vijayabahu I and left Sri Lanka for good. Throughout the remainder of the 11th and 12th Centuries, Polonnaruwa flourished as a sophisticated capital city and the islanders basked in affluence and political stability. Buddhism revived, the splendid palaces at Anuradhapura and the canals and reservoirs were restored, writers were encouraged and flourished; throughout the 12th Century, the land was blessed.

However, internal disputes, fomented by the Cholas and Pandyans, led to a crisis. There was no organised resistance when the pillaging crusades of a Tamil pirate named Magha – the Tiger – from the Indian state of Kalinga wreaked havoc over the cities and plains of the beautiful island. The old kings and their loyal subjects were driven always southwards, eventually to Jayavardhanapura (Kotte), near the modern capital of Colombo, on the south-west seaboard.

Magha died in 1255. The Sinhalese retreated into the rain forests in the central southern part of Sri Lanka, creating a natural geographical barrier between themselves and the Tamils, who colonised the Jaffna Peninsula in the Northern tip. The last Sinhalese King who was able to claim authority over the whole island was Parakramabahu VI (1411–1467) who ruled from Kotte.

Early in the 16th Century, the first Europeans arrived. These were Portuguese merchants anxious to offer the Sinhalese Catholicism in return for spices. They colonised the south-west third of the island, making a vassal of Don Juan Dharmapala, the legitimate King of Kotte. Nonetheless, armed resistance continued, notably under Vidiye Bandara, Mayadunne, and the great Rajasinghe I, King of Sitavaka.

The Kandyans in the hilly inland areas remained stubbornly independent and enlisted the support of the latest arrivals – the Dutch. In return for driving out the Portuguese, the Dutch would receive a monopoly of the spice trade. The Dutch expelled the Portuguese but decided, in defiance of all their treaties, to retain control over all the captured territory. Cinnamon had become hugely profitable: "The bride before whom all danced."

The merchants brought with them confusing varieties of Christianity. The Portuguese were Catholics, the Dutch Calvinists and the British, who followed the Dutch, Anglicans. Catholicism proved the most durable; today nine out of every ten Christians on the island are Catholic. Some English sailors, held hostage in Kandy and elsewhere, found conditions of life on the island preferable to the debilitating poverty back home and even when they were free to return stayed on.

By the Treaty of Amiens in 1802, all Dutch possessions on the island were handed over to the British and Frederick North became the first Governor. Only the brave Kandyans remained to be subdued; they held out bravely for a while but by 1805, the year of the Battle of Trafalgar, the might of the British East India Company had become irresistible. The Great Rebellion of 1817/18, inflamed in part by new levies and taxes, was a final gesture of defiance – but doomed.

This uprising evoked spontaneous support from all the Kandyan people, with the notable exception of the small Muslim community. It proved extraordinarily difficult for the British soldiers to counter guerilla tactics in the jungle; their resources too stretched and their knowledge of the country too limited, they adopted scorched earth tactics in an attempt to starve the rebels into submission. Local morale was further depressed with the capture by the British of the Sacred Tooth Relic, originally brought to the island in the 4th Century A.D. The Portuguese, who occupied Sri Lanka in 1505, announced that they had destroyed it in Goa but Buddhists insist that it miraculously saved itself. The rebellion eventually collapsed after the arrival of reinforcements from India.

To digress for a moment, one of the most memorable days David Hicks and I shared in Kandy was spent with Dr. Nissaka Wijeyeratne, who showed us almost every detail of the Temple. We were lucky indeed. Few know the Temple of The Tooth better than Lissanka – who had been Guardian of the Temple for several years; the highest office to which a lay Buddhist can be elected.

The highlight of our day was the ceremonial ascent of the steep wooden stairs leading into the Inner Shrine, wherein is kept the Tooth itself, enclosed on three sides by gilt iron bars firmly fixed to the back wall. These bars had been put in by the British, who showed a healthy respect for the relic; Mountbatten even mounted a 24-hour guard around the temple, for the Tooth's disappearance would be ominous for all. The sacred relic itself is enclosed in seven dagoba-shaped caskets, each of which is studded with fine gems and festooned with jewelled chains.

We three stood in silence before the shrine with our secret thoughts; one Sri Lankan (a Kandyan at that) and two Britishers, our island nations brought together first by invasion and conquest, stood now together as friends and partners joined by common causes.

Under the British, enlightened reforms were introduced. Catholic priests were permitted, as they had not been under the Dutch, to perform marriage and burial services. Laws hostile to the Muslim communities were repealed. A policy aimed at subsuming the old Kandyan kingdom within the Crown Colony of Ceylon was not entirely consistent with the philosophy of *laissez faire*, so that while the Kandyans retained their old habits of inheritance, caste, marriage and land tenure, in most other ways they became subjects of the Queen through the Governor. (The caste system was more amorphous than in India and the concept of Untouchability scarcely existed.) Rajakariya, or compulsory service for the king, was abolished in 1833, and the jury system was reformed ten years later. To discourage further rebellions and to facilitate trade, a network of roads opened up the hitherto impenetrable jungles. Along with the Sinhalese and any remaining Tamils, a Muslim community emerged among the Moors, who had been quietly – and rather profitably – minding their own business for some 500 years.

The Colebrooke-Cameron Commission recommended less cynical profiteering and a greater respect for local traditions. Civil servants were required to learn both Tamil and Sinhalese, a rule that became as common in the breach as in the observance. Plantations were laid out – no fewer than 130 in the five years from 1838 – coffee, tea, rubber and coconuts were introduced and the economy flourished. Immigrant labour was brought from the south of India to help with the harvesting.

Many of these newcomers found full-time employment and stayed, forming a disadvantaged urban proletariat. These India Tamils were, and are, quite distinct from the Jaffna Tamils, who had settled in Sri Lanka so many centuries before.

The most contentious issue was the traditional linking of the Sinhalese State with Buddhism. Regarded as quite unacceptable in London, the matter seemed very much less clear-cut to the Governors and Collectors in Ceylon.

In many ways, Ceylon was perceived as a constitutional experiment in the tolerant administration of a colony; those who planned it were not without idealism, and those who ran it were not without concern. A centralised administration was set up. With jurisdiction over the whole island, the judiciary was, and was seen to be, independent. Trial by jury was statutory. Only in the areas of education and religion were the new rulers implacable.

Education was put in the hands of missionaries, and missionary schools believed in conversion to Christianity as the cornerstone of education. It was not until the enlightened governorships of Sir William Gregory (1872–77) and Sir Arthur Gordon (1883–90) that the short-sightedness of these policies were perceived. Buddhism, which had been enjoying a revival, in part at least as a result of the campaign against it by the British, once more became central to the island's culture, the Government's strict neutrality in religious affairs was emphasized and a few members of the Kandyan nobility were given minor administrative roles.

Perhaps the British perceived that traditional values would help to preserve the status quo in a changing world; but it seems that there was a genuine curiosity amongst many colonial administrators when faced with cultures and traditions older and more profound than those in which they themselves had been brought up. It was a measure of the success of men like

Gregory and Gordon that by the end of the century it seemed that Ceylon would remain British for ever.

There were riots in 1915. Young Sinhalese radicals and nationalists marking the centenary of the loss of the Kandyan Kingdom attacked a group of Muslim merchants known as the Coast Moors. These were recent immigrants from the Malabar coast and they were unpopular because they were reputed to be keen and energetic money-lenders; their profit margins were also seen as excessive; *mutatis mutandis*! Worried that the riots might be directed against the Colonial authorities, the British authorities over-reacted, arresting and jailing prominent leaders, mostly Sinhalese Buddhists. The militant and radical Young Lanka League and trade union activists in the rail sheds in Colombo were also singled out for repressive treatment.

The 1920's saw the early signs of disaffection between Tamils and Sinhalese when the leaders of both communities seized the opportunity to make their voices heard before the Donoughmore Commission into Constitutional Reform, which was set up by the Colonial Office a century after the historic Colebrooke-Cameron Commission.

The Commission's report, a model of colonial administration, recommended a system of seven executive committees reporting to a State Council, a representation in miniature of the League of Nations Constitution. The Governor would retain reserve powers, but responsibility would be delegated to local politicians.

Against the wishes of a delegation from the Congress – consisting of President E.W. Perera with S.W.R.D. Bandaranaike and R.S.S. Gunawardene as joint secretaries – the Commission recommended voting rights for men over 21 and women over 30. (Up until then only some 4% of the population had been entitled to vote.) Remarkably, after studying the report the Colonial Office insisted that all men and women over 21 should be enfranchised. Thus Ceylon became not only the first British colony in Asia, but the first Asian country to enjoy universal suffrage, as well as elected ministers.

The report did not go down well in Ceylon however. The ethnic minorities, and especially the Tamils, were hostile to the idea of universal suffrage. Did it not mean that the Sinhalese would permanently hold the reins of power in the country? "I'll make Jaffna an Ulster and I'll be its Lord Carson," declared H.A.P. Sandarasagara. If the Tamils were hostile, the Sinhalese were no happier. They feared the new constitution would give the Indian migrant community a dangerous measure of power in the Central Highlands. Ironically, the only groups wholeheartedly to welcome the report were the Labour Union and the Unionist Association – the extreme left and the extreme right respectively.

What the report did achieve was to give respectability to the trade unionist, A.E. Goonesinha, and to help unite the Buddhist Nationalists. But it also divided its opponents into several splinter groups, of which the All-Ceylon Liberal League was the most influential. In time the Colonial Office realised that the Tamils, at least, deserved representation and the addition of four Tamil seats to the State Council was approved.

During the 1930's and 40's, a substantial rise in the price of tea and rubber helped to ease the burden of unemployment, which had dogged the island since the Great Depression (export revenue fell from 479 million rupees in 1927 to 189 million rupees five years later). The Depression had been followed by a disastrous malaria epidemic. A programme of social welfare was undertaken, with a national health service, a free school system and food subsidies. But the British made few attempts to introduce new industries, to plant new forests, to enrich the soil, to renovate the reservoirs, or to plough the vast profits from tea and rubber back into the land which produced them. Nevertheless, railways and macadamized roads were built and the ports of Colombo and Trincomalee improved.

Ceylon was to have a vital strategic role to play in the Second World War and – in contrast to India – it gave total commitment to the Allies. The ports of Colombo and Trincomalee were vital to both sides. In April 1942, Japan attacked and more than 1,000 troops and civilians died defending the island. Churchill's view was that this battle was the most crucial moment of the war. Had the island fallen to the Japanese, the Churchill Government would have fallen with it. And after that it is alarming to speculate what might have happened.

Mountbatten had never been happy having his headquarters in Calcutta. "Over-crowded, famine-ridden and full of objectionable troubles," he complained. The Americans and the Chiefs of Staff favoured a move to Delhi but Mountbatten as usual got his way, and in 1944 Kandy became his new headquarters. "The most beautiful spot in the world, and a delightful place in which to work," he wrote, and took as his residence the imposing King's Pavilion, setting up his staff in the Botanical Gardens. Mountbatten showed his gratitude with wholehearted support for Senanayake's Draft Constitution.

The transition to independent status was interrupted by the unexpectedly sudden surrender of the Japanese after the dropping of the atomic bombs on Hiroshima and Nagasaki and by the equally unexpected defeat of the Conservatives in Britain's General Election of 1945. Lord Soulbury had headed a Commission in Whitehall and this produced a report which Senanayake declared unacceptable. But with a new government and a new Colonial Secretary, G.H. Hall, Senanayake decided to raise the ante, and press for Dominion Status, imposed by an immediate Order-in-Council. Clement Attlee, Churchill's successor, was not persuaded. A White Paper on the Soulbury Commission was produced; this favoured the granting of Dominion Status, but remained vague about a time-scale for achieving it.

Indian and Burman self-rule was announced in February 1947, and yet another Colonial Secretary, Arthur Creech-Jones, seemed more receptive to Senanayake's persuasive powers than his predecessor. It is probable that the British Government realised that if Independence was too long delayed the radicals on the island might take matters into their own hands. For an orderly transfer of power, it was essential that political stability could continue. Therefore a date was agreed on the basis of Senanayake's original proposals, and Ceylon became Independent on 4th February 1948.

In India, the granting of Independence was greeted with massacres on a horrifying scale, and disturbances not far short of Civil War. In Burma, Aung San, who had negotiated the Treaty, was assassinated with several of his colleagues before Independence had been formally achieved. In Ceylon (as it still was) the change-over was peaceful, even amicable. As Sir Oliver Goonetelleke, who became Governor-General declared at the time: "To my British friends, I say 'Look on your handiwork and rejoice. You have built wisely elsewhere too; but perhaps nowhere else so well as in Ceylon.'"

Tamils came into the Cabinet, and the only dissident voices raised came from the Marxist factions, divided amongst themselves – as usual – by problems of ideology. But freedom of speech and assembly were assured, and regular elections on a multi-party basis guaranteed. Sri Lanka was a member of the Commonwealth of Nations and a founder member of the Non-Aligned Group.

Sri Lanka's recent history may be briefly told. D. S. Senanayake died in 1952, and was succeeded by his son, Dudley, at the head of the United National Party. S.W.R.D. Bandaranaike, a cabinet colleague of the late Prime Minister, left the UNP to found a new grouping, the Sri Lanka Freedom Party (S.L.F.P), which was to the left of the UNP, to the right of the Marxists, and which was able to count on the support of the Buddhists. In 1956, the SLFP won power at the elections and Bandaranaike became Prime Minister. But the election, which coincided with the 2,500th anniversary of the death of the Buddha, was marred by religious riots.

In 1959, Bandaranaike was murdered by a fanatic who had been one of his staunchest supporters in the election. The UNP was voted back into power for just a few weeks, when it was replaced by a Freedom Party, reorganised and strengthened by Bandaranaike's energetic widow, Sirimavo.

During her first term in office, Mrs. Bandaranaike came to an accord with the Indian Prime Minister, Lal Shastri, by which 500,000 Indian Tamils from Sri Lanka were exchanged for 300,000 Sri Lankan residents of India. She attempted to impose Sinhalese as the only national language for the island (with the effect that the Tamils became more than ever determined to use the Tamil language exclusively), and to bring all educational establishments under state control. She adopted a policy of nationalisation and formed an unhappy coalition with the Lanka Sama Samaja 'Equal Society' Party. She only just survived an attempted coup by officers from the army, the navy and the police, and in March 1965, was voted out of office, being replaced by Dudley Senanayake for his second term.

In 1970, in coalition with the Trotskyites and the pro-Moscow Communists, Mrs. Bandaranaike was once more voted into office. But it was in the following year that an ominous new organisation made its presence felt. Young radicals calling themselves the Janata Vimukti Peramuna – the JVP – resorted to violence in an attempted insurrection, failing to kidnap the Prime Minister and suffering many casualties. More than 10,000 members of the JVP were arrested.

Sir Evelyn Wrench, founder of the English-Speaking Union – 'What others have dreamed, he has done'.

Her Majesty the Queen meets Sir Evelyn Wrench as she signs the Visitors' Book of the Royal Overseas League.

His Highness Prince Nawab Mir Mohsin Ali Kahn of Hyderabad, patron of the ESU of South Asia.

President Jayawardene is presented with the first edition of Open Mind, the ESU of Sri Lanka's newspaper, by Michael Wynne-Parker. Also shown (from left to right) are Mr. A. Hathy Sulaiman, Dr. T. Amerasinghe and Mr. Abdul Ameer.

The launch of the ESU of Sri Lanka Appeal, Colombo, on 30th January 1989. Michael Wynne-Parker explains the target is 10 million rupees (about £170,000). Also pictured are Mr. Laksman Wijewardene and Dr. Amerasinghe.

Princess Ushi devi Rathore and Mr. Ahmed Jaffer at Dartmouth House for the first reception for the ESU of South Asia Council on 26th Septmember 1988.

Haritha Wijewardene receives his Oxford Summer School award certificate from President Jayawardene. His father, Laksman Wijewardene and A. Hathy Sulaiman – who helped find the ESU of Sri Lanka's first premises – look on.

The author (centre) introduces Dr. Terence Amerasinghe, President of the English-Speaking Union of Sri Lanka, to Foreign Secretary Sir Geoffrey Howe, patron of the Dartmouth House Appeal.

Rear Admiral Richard Heaslip, Director General of the English-Speaking Union, London, in the newly restored Dartmouth House.

The inaugural dinner of the ESU of Sri Lanka, at Dartmouth House, 3rd June 1982. From left to right, Sir Patrick Dean, Madame Moorthy, H. E. Aramba Moorthy – the High Commissioner – Miss Adele Abharatne, Dr. Terence Amerasinghe, Michael Wynne-Parker.

An informal glimpse of President Jayawardene's private residence, Ward Place, in Colombo. Also present are Mr. Laksman Wijewardene, Dr. Amerasinghe and the author.

HRH Prince Philip, President of the English-Speaking Union shares a joke with Group Captain David Hicks and Michael Wynne-Parker at the ESU's 70th anniversary celebrations at Dartmouth House in 1988.

President Premadasa, moments after he saved his predecessor J. R. Jayawardene from an assassination attempt in the Sri Lankan Parliament.

President Premadasa receiving Michael-Wynne Parker at Parliament Building. Also photographed (from left to right) are Ruwan Fonseka, Asitha Perera and Dr. Nissanka Wijeyeratne, all founder members of the ESU of Sri Lanka.

Partly as a result of these disturbances, the policy of nationalisation was speeded up, until no private agricultural enterprise survived. A new constitution was adopted and the name of the island was officially changed to Sri Lanka.

Perhaps inevitably, a balance of payments crisis followed. When quarrels within the Government on what economic measures were required became too disruptive, the Equal Society Party was expelled. Attempts to make concessions to the Tamils, now calling for an independent separatist state in the north – Eelaam – failed, and the Coalition disintegrated.

In the general election of 1977, the UNP won 140 out of 168 seats with a clear majority of the popular vote. Mrs. Bandaranaike's SLFP had its 90 seats reduced to 8, while the Marxists enjoyed not a single success.

The victory heralded a peaceful revolution, comparable to – if not greater than – the 1956 victory of the SLFP, which had changed both the education and administrative systems by making Sinhala the official language, introducing restrictive economic measures, nationalisation and overseeing the departure of British troops from the Trincomalee naval base.

Two decades later, the 1977 revolution of J. R. Jayawardene ushered in the Open Economic Policy, privatisation, the use of Tamil as a national language and English as a 'link' language.

From 1977 to 1983, the golden years seemed to return. Under the new constitution, J. R. became the country's first Executive President. Economic development gathered pace. Vast new construction works were undertaken, chief amongst which were the Victoria Dam and the Accelerated Mahaveli Project. The standard of living improved. In the realm of foreign affairs, Sri Lanka was poised to take the leadership of the smaller nations in South Asia, and ties with the West were resumed. The contrast between the lean Bandaranaike years and the hectic activity of the Jayawardene era was visible not merely to the masses in Sri Lanka but to the whole world.

A Tamil was Leader of the Opposition in Parliament; a Tamil was Attorney General; a Tamil was the Inspector General of Police, and a Tamil was to assume the highest legal post in the land, that of Chief Justice. The leader of the JVP was released from life imprisonment and the party acquired democratic aspirations.

It was under these favourable conditions that the Presidential Elections of 1982 took place. The candidates included both J.R. and Rohana Wijeweera, the JVP leader. The election was hard fought with J.R. being declared the winner and continuing the open policies of his last administration. During the early months of 1983, prosperity reached new heights. It seemed like a triumph, but it turned to tragedy. Destablisation followed.

Dissatisfied Tamil elements in the north, with South Indian assistance, turned from the ballot to the bullet. The new turn of events have so far defied solution. In June 1983, a Sinhalese backlash took place, and the impasse between Tamils and Sinhalas crystallised. The JVP abandoned its democratic pretensions and adopted a policy of violent confrontation. Development programmes were halted, although heroic efforts on the part of the Government and the contractors enabled the two major projects to be successfully completed.

But when the All-Party Conference failed to reach a consensus on a political solution to the Tamil problem, increased violence in the north resulted and rapidly spread to the east, "the rice-bowl of Sri Lanka". Although the Sri Lanka Freedom Party and its allies called for parliamentary elections, these could not be held in the face of terrorism. Instead a referendum was organised, and the Government Party received a fresh mandate. Many of the voters believed that, if Sri Lanka's unitary system were to continue, the UNP Government and its Executive President had to be in charge.

The tragic departure of Indira Gandhi from the Indian scene made possible the Thimpu talks with the Elamists, sponsored by the Indian Government. They promised much, but failed. Violence in the north grew worse. The President had little choice but to instruct the Army to impose a military solution. At a crucial moment in the campaign, the Indian Government sounded a note of warning by trespassing into the island's air space. President J.R.'s appeal to the Western nations for help went unregarded; it seems that disinformation by Elamist allies in those countries had been most effective. The President's westernised policy was in ruins.

The Peace Accord with India was signed by the Sri Lankan Government in September 1987. It got a mixed reception. The President and his supporters referred to it as a new Brest-Litovsk Treaty and quoted Lenin's 'Stoop To Conquer' speech of 1917. Opposition propaganda, however, found it difficult to come to terms with the new Accord, for friendship with India had always been *their* policy. Instead, they turned to sharp criticism of India's conduct.

As a result of the Accord, an Indian peace-keeping force was quartered in the north and the east of the island to contain Tamil terrorists, At first, the Tamils welcomed these Indians as liberators, but in time, their presence became yet another impediment to a peaceful political solution of the Tamil question.

Towards the end of 1988, with the President's term of office drawing to a close and his Excellency's firm commitment not to alter the Constitution – necessary if he were to stand again – the Presidential elections were held. What was virtually a straight fight between Ranasinghe Premadasa of the UNP and the SLFP's candidate, Sirimaro Bandaranaike, ensued. Contrary to the predictions of astrologers, seasoned diplomats and others, Premadasa was returned with an impressive majority. It was a victory for the common man; a Sri Lankan version of the Abraham Lincoln story, but the triumphant progress was from Kehelwatte to Temple Trees, not from log cabin to White House.

Further parliamentary elections in February 1989 confirmed that it was the wish of the majority that UNP rule should continue and the opposition parties were only saved from a complete rout by J. R. Jayawardene's introduction of proportional representation, a constitutional reform bitterly contested by the SLFP.

Both before and after the 1989 elections, there was a remarkable closing of ranks in the UNP. An attempt on JR's life was certainly partly responsible for this. As he described it to me, the assassination attempt took place within the precincts of Parliament. The Prime Minister (now the President) was at his side. He remembers looking down at his notes – then a blank. Seconds later, he found himself under the table, pressed down by President Premadasa, who had apparently seen a grenade thrown through the door and bouncing across the room. He had grabbed J.R.'s arm and pulled him under the table, thus saving his life.

In the deeply religious atmosphere of Sri Lanka such events are considered "providential" and the perceived bond between the former and present Presidents seems likely to survive, even in the brittle climate of Sri Lankan politics. Such a bond is not only of inestimable value to the UNP, to which they both belong, but to the continued preservation of the territorial integrity of the country.

Since the general election – and the victory of moderation over unreason – the atmosphere in Sri Lanka has become more tranquil. There are occasional curfews and necessary restrictions, but life goes on.

I was discussing one evening with Dr. Amerasinghe what

might happen if Sri Lanka were to become a Marxist dictatorship. "Of course," I said, "I shall be in serious trouble with my business interests, but what about the ESU?"

Amerasinghe replied that even on a Marxist island, the ESU would be welcome, though the suggestion that Sri Lanka could become another Cuba is flying in the face of history. The JVP supporters pose a serious threat. There are plenty of them. They have no compunction about killing others and they seem perfectly prepared to be killed themselves. But they have no quarrel with us. We are offering a commodity which everybody needs if they are to communicate successfully, whatever their religion or philosophy.

Chapter 6

THE ENGLISH-SPEAKING UNION: FOUNDATION AND SURVIVAL

"The hope of the City of God at the other end of the road."

John Masefield

On 1st August 1914, Evelyn Wrench was spending the day quietly enjoying a visit to Pickwick country. He rambled about the battlements of Rochester Castle ("Magnificent ruin," said Jingle. "Fine place . . . glorious pile . . . frowning walls . . . tottering arches . . . dark nooks . . . crumbling staircases.") and then ordered chops, fried potatoes and apple tart at the Bull Inn, where the Pickwick Club were wont to dine.

But the chops were going to have to wait. A telegram arrived from Northcliffe:

> *"Return at once and come round to Printing House Square. France mobilising."*

Reluctant as he was to leave his blossoming Overseas Club, Northcliffe proposed that Wrench should take charge of the Paris Daily Mail. Evelyn agreed. The comment in his diary is poignant: "It is so extraordinary suddenly changing all one's plans and spending most of the night rushing round to Passport offices. The only time I ever had a passport before was in Russia and Turkey. This morning, when dawn was breaking, I motored along the empty streets and saw the Cross of St. Paul's standing out wonderfully against a pink sky."

Evelyn did as he was told and went to Paris. There, war fever was becoming an epidemic. Huge crowds were carrying tri-colours through the streets and singing the Marseillaise. Less admirably they were looting German shops and breaking the windows of German-owned cafes. Mobilising troops swarmed through the Gare de L'Est.

On 5th August, London announced that, as a result of the German's violating Belgium neutrality, Great Britain was now at war with Germany. Overnight, Paris turned Anglophile. Cries of "Hurrah pour L'Angleterre" and "Vivent Les Anglais" echoed round the boulevards. But the disconsolate Americans besieged their Embassy, as they tried to beat the red tape and get home. It was a curious time to find oneself in Paris and Wrench felt powerfully that he would be more usefully employed in London "organising Empire sentiment".

He was anxious – but not desperately so – when news came through that his father, mother and sister had been detained by the German authorities at Bad Nauheim.

Meanwhile, the British Expeditionary Force landed, the French occupied Alsace and the newspapers were full of headlines like "German troops defeated by Belgians", "Twenty-five German ships captured", and "German Peril in Liege". The only trouble was nobody thought to tell the Germans that they were being defeated, and within a couple of weeks the news was very different. The German occupation of Brussels could not be gainsaid.

By 24th August, Wrench was back in London. His heart had never really been in his work for the Paris Daily Mail, and when the newspaper (and the French Government) moved to Bordeaux, he came home. Now his patriotism became obsessive and he wrote that his "real" religion was the British Commonwealth. He made heroes of those who displayed the right degree of patriotic fervour – Cecil Rhodes, Lord Curzon, Joseph Chamberlain, and Theodore Roosevelt amongst others. The rolling phrases of Lord Curzon in particular pleased him mightily: "As the years roll by, the call seems to me more clear, the duty more imperative, the work more magnetic, the goal more sublime. To me, the message is carved in granite, it is hewn out of the rock of doom – that our work is righteous and that it shall endure."

The opportunities offered by the war for forging stronger bonds with the Empire were not to be wasted, and the offices of the Overseas Club in the Aldwych became central to his plans. There, as he recorded, he was visited by "farmers from the Canadian West or Queensland, banana and coffee planters from the West Indies, fruit growers from the Transvaal and New Zealand, miners of diamonds, gold, coal and iron from South Africa, British Columbia and West Australia, ostrich farmers from Natal, lighthouse-keepers from lonely outposts on the high seas, sheep-shearers from the great Australian plains, cattle-hands from Rhodesia, officers and men in the Merchant Service – it was a marvellous medley from the Seven Seas".

Baden-Powell was impressed and spoke of the possibility of the Boy Scout movement affiliating. The only difference between the two organisations, he reckoned, was that "one was for grown ups and the other for the growing-ups".

Organising was Wrench's forte. No sooner was the idea mooted for an Overseas Club Tobacco Fund for the troops than, with Wrench's guiding hand, it became a reality. Vast sums were raised so that Tommy in the trenches could enjoy his fags; over a quarter of a million children gave pennies in 1916 alone. No sooner, it seemed, did he conceive the idea of an Overseas Aircraft Flotilla, than he had raised £100,000 and presented to the Royal Flying Corps aircraft bearing such evocative names as *Victoria, Hong Kong, Nova Scotia, Saskatchewan, Shanghai Race Club, The Springbok, Mount Lofty* and *A Devil Bird from Ceylon*.

Evelyn Wrench's cousin, Lady des Voeux, came in as a staunch chairman of the Soldiers and Sailors Fund, which distributed gifts of all sorts to serving troops. Requests were received for items as varied as fingerless gloves for men on tank vessels and minesweepers, and rosaries, while gifts for distribution included barber's kits and a ventriloquist's dummy. Beds were provided for many of the Red Cross Hospitals.

In the summer of 1916, Wrench wrote about a visit he paid to the Star and Garter Home at the top of Richmond Hill, where it still proudly stands: "It is the memory of the poor fellows lying on their backs that I carried away. After leaving the Star and Garter I walked across to Richmond Park and sat on a chair near the gate. A company of Scots Guards out drilling marched by. I shut my eyes and listened to their regular step in perfect unison crunching the gravel. They walked so erect and they looked so full of life. What a contrast to the occupants of the beds just across the road."

Hylda des Voeux, who worked so hard for the causes which Evelyn Wrench espoused was to be rewarded in 1937, when having been widowed, she found herself free to marry the man she so deeply admired. It had been a long-standing friendship. In 1908, he had lodged with Sir Frederick and Hylda des Voeux. The plan had been for him to stay six months with them; he stayed four years. In his first autobiography 'Uphill', published in 1934, he describes her thus: "Riches and ambition as a goal were beyond her comprehension, a burning Faith was the mainspring of her life, she lived for others. She was a devoted mother . . . She awoke my interest in poetry and botany. She lived in a world of books. There was hardly a biography about a saint or mystic, literary celebrity or poet she had not read."

Wrench settled down in a service flat at 87, Victoria Street, where he was to live for the next 14 years. As stories drifting back from the various battle fronts became more and more gruesome, he found it hard to believe that the Germans could have been guilty of such atrocities. "I knew that my German friends couldn't overnight become a race of savages. . . Even if a case could be made out against the German High Command in the matter of the Belgian atrocities, what had the poor hard-working, self-respecting German lads whom I saw as prisoners in France and England to do with the nightmare of war in which they found themselves?". The use of mass hatred and emotive language to inflame passions against one's enemies was a trend which he observed increasingly in the newspapers and increasingly deplored.

The news from the front became more and more depressing. Those who knew about such things realised that the Battle of Jutland was by no means the great naval victory that had been so passionately anticipated; the Germans destroyed nearly twice the tonnage and more than double the number of men that they themselves lost. Wrench was asked to help with the recruitment drive and did so. But he was entering a period of spiritual barrenness which lasted throughout 1915.

And yet the war had started well for Wrench. An historic meeting with Walter Hines Page, the American Ambassador at the Court of St. James, resulted in the idea of an English-Speaking Union or Brotherhood. King George V became Patron of the Overseas Club and Alexander Smith Cochrane, an American multi-millionaire, chipped in with £1,000 for furnishing the premises when it had begun to seem likely that visitors would have to sit on the floor. "Once this darned war is over and I quit being a neutral," said the Ambassador, "I will help you to get a million members for your show in the U.S.A."

It was not to be. In October 1918, shortly after the foundation of the English-Speaking Union, Walter Hines Page left England and died two months later. But his influence lived on. "If there be estrangement between the British Empire and the United States after the war," he said shortly before his death, "God pity the world." His years in England had been blighted by America's refusal to enter the war, despite the sinking of the *Lusitania*.

Standing on the ticket of keeping America out of the war, Woodrow Wilson defeated Teddy Roosevelt in 1916, and entered his second term of office. It was a blow to the British war effort, and a blow to the imperial ambitions of Evelyn Wrench.

In May 1915, the secret of Kitchener's mismanagement of the war effort became a matter of public concern when the Daily Mail published its famous headline: "The Shells Scandal: Lord Kitchener's tragic blunder". Northcliffe's attacks on the brass hats had its consequences. The Daily Mail was burned on the floor of the Stock Exchange, there was talk of applying the Defence of the Realm Act to muffle the Mail and the politicians became heated, but Lloyd George knew the truth of the allegations and he was a most powerful ally. No action was taken against the "defeatist" Mail.

By then, with a further generous donation from Cochrane, Evelyn Wrench had started Overseas, his Empire magazine with an elegant cover designed by Macdonald Gill, depicting a sailing ship, called "Overseas" sailing towards the rising sun. Early contributors included the King, the Prince of Wales, Bernard Shaw, Sir Harry Lauder and A.A. Milne.

April saw the first German gas attack on the men in the trenches. In May, the first Overseas Plane was delivered to the R.F.C. The autumn saw a wave of Zeppelin attacks on London and the disastrous Dardanelles Campaign which culminated in the evacuation of Gallipoli in January 1916, a defeat which was hailed by the British, like Dunkirk in the second World War, as a victory. The Easter Rising and the fall of Kut exacerbated the situation. What with howitzers and Zeppelins and poison gas, it seemed as though the initiative in the war effort was conclusively with the Germans.

But September saw the first use of tanks by the British Army on the Somme. Their effect was small in terms of material advantage, but huge in raising the morale of the troops. And when at the end of the year Lloyd George was asked to head a new Government, it seemed as though good times were, as the song insisted, just around the corner. Basil Clarke, the war correspondent, wrote to Overseas in even more buoyant mood: "Our boys' task is difficult, but Fritz's task is well-nigh impossible. So convinced am I of this that the end will come before Autumn 1917 – if only we buckle to and put in every ounce of our weight."

A war correspondent should have known better. It would be a year before the battle of Paschendale.

Although he was sure that the work he was doing in the Aldwych offices was of greater importance than getting into uniform, he informed the War Office that he was available for any work "of greater use to the country than that on which I am already engaged". The call came in 1917, and Wrench applied for a commission in the Kite Balloon Section in France, to be told that the Royal Flying Corps wanted him to work as an organiser in London. With a touch of asperity he remarked that instead of working for the nation in an honorary capacity he was now to receive a subaltern's pay.

The following month America entered the war.

The spring of 1917 found Evelyn Wrench touring Scotland and looking for likely young recruits for the R.F.C. He was shocked by the poverty, squalour and drunkenness he observed – and almost as shocked by the appalling discomfort he experienced in provincial hotels. Worse was to come. He was ordered to Reading to complete his training in the mysteries of aeroplane construction and the internal combustion engine. He became, he wrote, "a human robot" and showed no flair for mechanical matters. "I fear the tax-payer got bad value for his money." But he was impressed that there was so little "smut" talked and was alarmed when a young woman he had met casually in the street invited him to go punting with her.

His course at Reading over, he celebrated with lobster and

devilled chicken washed down with Burgundy at Scott's of Coventry Street – where else?

The hard training he had undergone was an inappropriate preface to the job selected for him, a desk job with the Air Board based at the 1,000-room Hotel Cecil. Here he learned the first rule of the good bureaucrat – the vital importance of initials. Was he A.D.D.M.A.D. or was he A.D.D.A.A.? In either case it seemed that he was working for the Directorate of Aircraft Acceptance . . . or was it the Military Aeronautics Directorate? His job was to organise the collection of completed planes from the manufacturers and make sure there were pilots available to ferry them to G.H.Q. in France. These pilots were "heroes, everyone of them" and furthermore: "to listen to their modest and unvarnished accounts of 'strafing the Hun' was an unforgettable experience".

Evelyn Wrench quickly grew accustomed to uniform and he recorded that there was no second-lieutenant who clicked his heels louder or who stood more correctly to attention when passed in the corridor by a superior officer than he. Within five months he had been promoted to Captain. And the department grew apace as the significance of air power became universally acknowledged. "It was curious," he wrote, "to lead a double existence: during the day as part of the military machine with its trappings and privileges; in the evening as the organiser of an Empire movement."

In November 1917, Lord Rothermere was appointed Air Minister, so that once more he was Wrench's chief. On 4th December, Rothermere selected Wrench to be his Private Secretary. "It was the first really happy thing that has taken place for a long while", he wrote. "It means that I have now got a really important job which will put me right in the centre of things." The day before, a Sunday, he had experienced a serious shock to his system: "I went into Miss K.'s room next door, she was also up doing Sunday work and I found her doing her typing and smoking a cigarette; just think, a lady secretary in a government office smoking! What are we coming to?"

With the news of the Bolshevist *coup d'etat* in Russia and the subsequent Armistice on the Russian front, and with America's entry into the war delayed until the spring, he was gloomy about the prospects for an early victory.

Although he enjoyed the importance and influence of working for Rothermere, he would have much preferred it if in public his boss spoke less about reprisals and more about ideals. In February 1918, Rothermere suffered a desperate personal tragedy. He had already lost one son, and now his eldest boy, Vyvyan Harmsworth, died of blood poisoning as a result of his war wounds. At a time when he felt he could have been of the greatest use and comfort to Rothermere, Wrench was struck down by mumps, and before he could get back to work, Rothermere was at the centre of continuing rows involving Beaverbrook, Churchill and Lloyd George and, close to a nervous breakdown, had resigned. His successor, Sir William Weir, appointed his own staff and Wrench was once more kicking his heels, his only souvenirs of the Hotel Cecil months a gold-leafed cap and an obscure honour – the Order of St. Maurice and St. Lazarus.

He did not kick his heels for long, and found himself appointed to Beaverbrook's Ministry of Information, where he was officially second in command to Lord Rothermere in his capacity as Controller for the Dominions and the United States. But since Rothermere never appeared at the Ministry, the running of wartime propaganda in the Dominions devolved almost entirely upon Major Wrench. Two writers worked as his colleagues in propaganda; Ian Hay collaborated on the USA and Arnold Bennett took responsibility for France.

There was no time to worry over-much about the morals of,

and motives for, wartime propaganda. It was generally understood that if the British people had been told the truth at the end of April 1917, that nearly a million tons of shipping had been sunk within the month and that there was just a month's supply of wheat left with which to feed the population, they would not have had the heart for the continuing struggle.

But those grim days were past. By July more than a million American "doughboys" had been landed in Europe. To Wrench the symbolic importance of the English-speaking nations fighting side by side against a common enemy could not be overstated. And the nature of his work ensured that he could be officially working on behalf of his two obsessions, Empire unity and British/American entente. He had no longer any need to put aside until the week-ends those ideas which thronged his waking consciousness. He was fully engaged.

He met prominent American and Canadian servicemen, senators, congressmen, university presidents and professors, editors and war correspondents, preachers, lecturers and popular entertainers. He agreed passionately with Walter Hines Page when he claimed that the ending of 140 years of hostility between the English-speaking nations was "the most momentous fact in the history of either people". Within a month of joining the Ministry of Information he had launched the English-Speaking Union, a title which he used first in his diary entry for 12th June 1918.

Wrench was often asked to explain the distinction between the Overseas League and the English-Speaking Union, and always answered that it was fundamental: membership of the League was confined to British subjects and existed to promote unity amongst the peoples of the Empire, whilst the essential purpose of the Union in those early days was to bring together the British Empire and North America in democratic amity.

In the first issue of a weekly publication called 'Land and

Water', Wrench wrote of "a great chain of fellowship which will encircle the globe" and continued: "In New York and London we envisage great buildings, with the comforts of a well-equipped club, with newspaper rooms containing all the leading journals of the English-speaking world, with a library of many of the greatest works telling of the history of the English-speaking peoples, with a lecture hall open to every movement dedicated to the services of the English-speaking peoples and of humanity."

In an article for the Observer (17th November 1918) these purposes were extended to include the interchange of visits by private individuals, professors, preachers, and sportsmen. Three days after this he added in an article in The Teacher's World that he also proposed an annual exchange of 100,000 school-children between the old world and the new, along with their teachers.

The founding dinner of the Union took place on 28th June in a private dining room at the Marlborough Club, overlooking Pall Mall. Wrench had invited fifteen guests: Algernon Aspinall, an authority on the West Indies, Boylston Beal, private secretary to Walter Hines Page, Ian Hay Beith and John Buchan, the writers, Professor McNeile Dixon, a colleague at the Ministry of Information, the Rev W.F. Geikie-Cobb, the rector of St. Ethelburga's, Bishopsgate, Sir Arthur Herbert, a distinguished diplomat, Francis Jones, from the Overseas League, James Keeley, a journalist from Chicago, George Mills McKay, a City merchant, the Australian Henry Noyes, Francis F. Powell, Chairman of the American Chamber of Commerce in London, A. Lyle-Samuel, Sir George Sutton, Chairman of the Amalgamated Press, and Fullerton Waldo, on the staff of the Philadelphia Public Ledger.

After dinner, Evelyn outlined the scheme and invited each guest to give his response in a five-minute address. Support was unanimous and a small steering committee was formed.

Influential men, including Winston Churchill and the young Franklin D. Roosevelt, were enrolled as Vice Presidents. Offices were leased in Howard Street just 50 yards away from the Ministry of Information and more or less opposite the Overseas Club. Money was readily forthcoming – £1,000 each from Colonel Astor, later Lord Astor of Hever, Alexander Smith Cochran and Sir Thomas Latham of Courtaulds, and significant sums from Lord Northcliffe, Walter S. Burns, the nephew of Pierpont Morgan, Robert Grant Jnr., Sir William Berry, later Lord Camrose, Jimmy White, a boxing promoter, Solly Joel, Claude Johnson of Rolls-Royce, A. Lyle-Samuel M.P., F.E. Powell, Gordon Selfridge, Sir Francis Trippel and Sir George Mills Mckay.

Since the aim was personal contact, Wrench organised a card index of all those who would be prepared to invite visitors to Britain to stay in their homes. M.P.s were asked to act as hosts and provide tea on the House of Commons terrace to Americans and plans were advanced for practitioners in different professions to meet their opposite numbers across the Atlantic.

After such a burst of energy, Wrench contracted a bout of influenza and went to Hertfordshire to recuperate. On his return he found that London had become a great clearing-house. As the war seemed to be nearing its happy conclusion, American statesmen and congressmen, journalists and editors arrived by the train-load, and it fell to Wrench to make them welcome. His position in the Government meant that he could entertain lavishly at the taxpayers' expense, at the Ritz or the Carlton or the Cheshire Cheese, and he organised a series of small dinner parties for influential visitors, amongst them General Smuts, Dr. Jowett, the Master of Balliol, Owen Seaman and others. Twelve Englishmen would be sandwiched between twelve Americans. On 11th October, Lord Balfour welcomed a party of American newspaper editors at a Criterion dinner organised by the English-Speaking Union. This was the occasion when, looking round the table, Wrench felt for the first time that his idea had assumed concrete reality. It was a success.

Exactly a month later on a drizzling November day, the maroons sounded to tell Londoners that, following discussions between General Foch and the German envoys, the war was finally over.

When President Woodrow Wilson came to London in December on his way to the Peace Conference and was greeted at Charing Cross by George V, a direct descendant of George III, Wrench wrote that it was a landmark in the history of the English-speaking world. It was the first time that the President of the Union and the King of England had ever been on the same continent, let alone together on the same railway station.

Such an opportunity was not to be missed, and Wrench led a small deputation of the Central Committee of the English-Speaking Union to meet the President at the Embassy in Grosvenor Gardens.

Wrench thus defined the purpose of the Union to Woodrow Wilson: "The English-Speaking Union . . . has been founded in no narrow attitude of race pride, in no spirit of hostility to any people. It does not aim at formal alliances, nor has it anything to say to the relationship of governments. It is simply a movement to draw together in the bonds of comradeship the English-speaking peoples of the world."

Woodrow Wilson's response was delivered with a twinkle in the eye: "Just because we do speak the same language and can read in each other's papers what is said about us on the opposite side of the Atlantic, we should be very careful what we say about one another!"

Early in the New Year, Major Wrench was officially discharged from the army – although he was allowed to retain his officer's rank. His work at the Ministry of Information had come to an end and he was no longer employed at the Daily Mail, so he was in the enviable position of being an entirely free man.

In February, the English-Speaking Union amalgamated with the Atlantic Union, an event which was celebrated with a lunch at which Lord Bryce took the chair, although it appears that he was completely inaudible. Not so the founder, who "spoke for about seven minutes . . . and I think I stirred things up a bit." ESU activities followed in quick succession; a Washington Birthday Dinner with Churchill in the chair, a lecture by Oliver Locker-Lampson about his experiences with armoured cars in Russia, a memorial service at Westminster Abbey in honour of American soldiers and sailors who died in the war and the preparation of an illuminated address to the American people.

At the Overseas Club, a debate was organised on the subject of prohibition. W. E. 'Pussyfoot' Johnson, the prophet of Prohibition and the doyen of the Anti-Saloon League, was to put the case for a "dry" society. Mr. Mitchell Banks would oppose. 'Pussyfoot' was seen in many quarters as a sinister figure whose intent was – in Horatio Bottomley's phrase – "to deprive the British working man of his beer".

Students from London University, from King's and Guy's and Bart's, decided they had an obligation to intervene. As the principal speakers – together with F.A. Mackenzie and Evelyn Wrench – mounted the platform at the Essex Hall they were greeted with shouts of: "What won the war? Beer!" Bags of flour were thrown and 'Pussyfoot' was kidnapped, carried in triumph to the yard of King's College and offered some beer, which he refused. He was then carried on a stretcher through the West End, until the police took a hand. In the resulting scuffles, a stone struck Johnson in the eye and he was taken to Bow Street Station for first aid. He was quoted as remarking – generously in the circumstances: "Tell the boys there is no ill will on my side, not a grain."

Even after his eye was removed he refused to complain, adding merely that: "The benefits which I believe have accrued to the cause we have at heart more than outweigh my sense of personal injury through the loss of an eye."

But Wrench was desolated that this unfortunate affair should have taken place as a result of a meeting organised by the Overseas Club. His own view on the issue was that it would not be long before the entire English-speaking world followed the example of the United States and went dry. Later he realised he had entirely underestimated the evils which Prohibition brought in its wake; smuggling, lawlessness and bootlegging.

"The best way of fighting the evil of drunkenness," he added, "is to reform the public house, to serve food with drink in pleasant surroundings, above all to give the people better housing conditions. I am still of the opinion that there should be public ownership of the drinks trade."

Early in 1920, the headquarters of the English-Speaking Union moved to Trafalgar Buildings, overlooking Trafalgar Square, with a view over what Lord Palmerston called: "The finest site in Europe". It was more costly than the organisation could properly afford, but John Astor came to the rescue with a donation of £1,000 and contracts were exchanged. A further unexpected donation of $4,000 from the ever-generous Alexander Smith Cochrane gave the Union an unusual measure of short-term financial stability. Soon afterwards, Wrench travelled to Oxford to present the University with £20,000 to endow a Chair of American History. The money had been given by Lord Rothermere in memory of his son Vyvyan.

In New York, a violent quarrel had broken out between two prominent members of the Provisional Committee, and things escalated to a point where both William Taft, ex-President, and Dr. Judson of Chicago University, withdrew their support. Wrench set off to try to heal the breach.

The crossing on the *Carmania* was not without incident. Evelyn was startled to observe a black American Army Officer with a white wife and half-caste child. "I feel very sorry for him and want to talk to him," he observed. Despite blizzards and gales he succeeded in enrolling 31 passengers as members of the English-Speaking Union.

In America he found an isolationist mood, which was distinctly unfriendly to European interests. President Wilson was in disfavour; it was thought that he had been outmanoeuvred by Lloyd George and Clemenceau at the Peace Conference. How could he have agreed to a League of Nations in which the British Empire would have six votes to America's one? And why were not the Europeans more grateful for America's altruistic intervention which had cost her 300,000 casualties and resulted in substantial debts? In such an atmosphere, exacerbated by American identification with the Irish rebels, there was little chance that the ideals of an organisation dedicated to Anglo-American co-operation would be sympathetically received. One man in Philadelphia told Wrench that "to admit ever having drunk a cup of afternoon tea was considered treason to the American Constitution!"

But Evelyn Wrench's energy and charm were insatiable. Dr. Judson, Dean of Chicago University, agreed to withdraw his resignation. Ex-President Taft agreed to remain President of the American branch of the ESU. But the high-spot of the trip was a dinner given at the University Club in New York where the Union was re-constituted as "an independent but Sister Society, working in the closest touch with the British Society."

On the return journey, despite being unnerved by seeing a large rat in the lavatory opposite his cabin, he surpassed himself and enrolled a further 60 members for the English-Speaking Union.

Back in England a period of acute depression followed. Isolationism and the Irish Question seemed insuperable barriers to Anglo-American understanding. It was ten years since Wrench had started the Overseas League and he was no longer convinced that individuals could alter the destiny of nations. Without the influence bestowed on him by the Daily Mail and the Ministry of Information he found it hard to pull necessary strings. It was comparatively easy to start a crusade, but to maintain the enthusiasm of founding fathers for fund-raising and humdrum committee work was a very different matter. He concluded: "Enthusiasm is evanescent. The paucity of result compared with the dream is baffling. The joy of service must be sufficient reward. He must not for ever be measuring up life's journey with a tape measure. He must get a true sense of values by withdrawing from the practical world to the realm of the spirit."

Despite these gloomy prognostications, the English-Speaking Union and the Overseas League survived – and Sir Evelyn Wrench survived into old age to see that the dream was as substantial as the enthusiasm of the man who had dreamed it. In the 1920's, Wrench acted in a dual capacity; he was secretary of the Overseas League and edited its monthly journal and he was twice elected Chairman of the English-Speaking Union.

In 1925, he bought a controlling interest in the Spectator, which he edited, and even after he sold out to Sir Ian Gilmour he remained Chairman of the Board until his death in 1966.

In 1930, he founded a third organisation, the All Peoples Association, dedicated to encouraging people to live in harmony. He laid the emphasis especially on Anglo-German entente, but there could hardly have been a less propitious time for such an enterprise. In 1940, he published a book poignantly entitled: "I Loved Germany", but this too was possibly misconceived. Certainly, it was misunderstood. In the same year Evelyn and Hylda undertook a tour of North America and Australasia. Stranded in India on their way home they did all they could for the G.I.s there, and Lord Linlithgow, the Viceroy, whom Nehru charmingly described as "solid as a rock and with almost a rock's lack of awareness", appointed Wrench to the newly-created post of American Relations Officer to the Government of India.

After the war, Evelyn moved with Hylda to the charming Mill House, in Marlow, where he concentrated on his writing. (Earlier, in 1934, he had completed the second instalment of his autobiography, 'Struggle: 1914–20'.) Besides 'Immortal Years: 1937–1944, as viewed from Five Continents' (1945), he published 'Transatlantic London: three centuries of association between England and America' (1949), and three biographies. 'Francis Yeats-Brown' (1948) was the life of Wrench's first cousin, the author of 'Bengal Lancer'. 'Geoffrey Dawson and our Times' (1955) told the story of the editor of the Times, who was given such a hard time by Lord Northcliffe. And 'Alfred Lord Milner: The Man of No Illusions' (1958), a biography of the colonial statesman and member of Lloyd George's War Cabinet. In his choice of subjects Wrench was certainly consistent. All had been personal friends and each one believed in the Commonwealth of Nations.

Hylda died in 1955. In 1958, Evelyn founded the Anglo-Kin Society to help provide topographical, historical, genealogical and geographic information to those wishing to do research in Great Britain. He was President of the Dickens Fellowship (1961–1964) and Senior Trustee of the Cecil Rhodes Memorial Museum at Bishop's Stortford. He had been knighted in 1932 and later became a KCMG.

Life is full of surprises. On a warm summer's day in 1988, I took Rear Admiral Richard Heaslip to lunch at the Carlton Club. I saw Robert Linsley, the Club Secretary, as we entered and introduced Dick to him. I learned that Mr. Linsley had been House Manager and General Club Manager at the Royal Overseas Services League for 21 years – between 1957 and

1978. I was face to face with one of the few people who knew Evelyn Wrench *really* well.

I asked Mr. Linsley how he would sum up Wrench's life in one sentence and he spontaneously replied: "He was the greatest idealist and most successful beggar I have ever met."

Very appropriately, Robert Linsley played a major role in the organisation of Sir Evelyn's Memorial Service which was held in the crypt of St. Paul's Cathedral. Many of Wrench's friends attended to represent the two organisations for which he will always be remembered: the English-Speaking Union and the Royal Overseas League.

During Sir Evelyn's declining years and, more importantly, following his death, the work of the ESU continued to develop both in America and the UK. The American ESU currently has 89 branches – the largest world member, with a permanent headquarters in New York. Sinclair Armstrong is the President and Paul Robinson, the former US Ambassador to Canada, the more recently appointed Chairman.

The ESU of the Commonwealth has been led by figures of international importance, from Winston Churchill (Chairman 1923–25) to the present time, when the English-Speaking Union has been fortunate to secure the services of Francis Pym as Chairman, bringing with him not only long parliamentary experience but also a record of distinguished service, both as Secretary of State for Northern Ireland and as Foreign Secretary. Much has been achieved in advancing Wrench's original aims, especially in Britain, where, after all, the ESU was founded.

Prominent amongst its varied activities here has been the annual Churchill lecture, given by an international statesman, the Oxford Summer School, innumerable educational programmes and student exercises at home and abroad, the schools' public speaking competitions at local and national level, literary gatherings to launch many a major new volume, concerts, debates and seminars. And all this supported by a network of branches throughout the country and led at the present time by the National Chairman, Peter Sparling. Gradually, I became aware of all of these strands, as I participated increasingly in the national affairs of the ESU, through my election to the National Council for England and Wales.

I was impressed at Dartmouth House by the enormous dedication of an underpaid staff who achieved so much. But despite the tremendous programme of activities, I detected a growing concern that all was not well with the finances. Whilst the work thrived, and I became more and more engaged with the work of the ESU abroad, the economics of the Union at home seemed to go from bad to worse. We had been living beyond our income.

We were close to panic stations when Sir Donald Tebbit, a distinguished diplomat and the kindest of men, who was Chairman of the ESU of the Commonwealth at that time, persuaded of the seriousness of the situation, convened a working party in October 1983. Its brief was: "To review the whole operation of the Union, both short and long term, in the light of the budget, the extent of our liabilities, the value and use of our assets, the income actually and potentially arising from them; and to make recommendations."

I was invited by Donald to serve on the sub-committee of the working party under the chairmanship of Alexander Macmillan (now Lord Stockton). Our object could be summed up in two words: Radical Solutions. I accepted the invitation with alacrity.

Our committee met regularly throughout the winter of 1983, and it soon became apparent that the majority was in favour of putting Dartmouth House on the market. With the substantial sums raised – and unless they were substantial no sale would proceed – the debts could be cleared and the balance spent on more modest premises and the setting up of an endowment fund. But there were three members of the committee rigorously opposed to such a draconian plan: Anthony Westnedge, Alison Wheatcroft and myself. Later we were joined by Rose Luce, the wife of the present Arts Minister and by Anne Chilton. Having discussed the enormous potential of Dartmouth House and its considerable assets (which include the Chesterfield Hotel) we decided to approach the Governors and do all we could to persuade them to change course.

Dartmouth House is – of course – the ESU's one tangible and considerable asset. It is situated at 37 Charles Street, and epitomises that most distinguished street in Mayfair, that most distinguished area of London. The Rev. Sydney Smith lived at number 32, and it was he who penned what might have been the ESU motto during those difficult times: "Poverty is no disgrace to a man, but it is confoundedly inconvenient."

Number 16 was the very pukka Guards Club and epitomised the whole area – vast 18th Century houses with plain but aristocratic frontages and sumptuous interiors. Dartmouth House used to be three houses, but was converted into a single mansion in 1980, by Lord Revelstoke. Representing the most solid virtues of the great period of Britain's imperial expansion, Charles Street is symbolically apt for the headquarters of the ESU.

Bernard Hollowood's words, published in Punch on the last day of 1952, are very apt: "A visit to the English-Speaking Union headquarters at Dartmouth House, Charles Street, London, can be almost embarrassingly uplifting and stimulating; for here the cement is Grade A and bonds of true and lasting friendship are being forged before one's very eyes."

It would surely have been a tragedy to let go of Dartmouth House while there was any chance of saving it.

In January 1984, at about the same time as his father in the

House of Lords was castigating the Conservative Party for "selling the family silver", Alex Macmillan reported to Sir Donald in these terms: "While it is the view of three members of the sub-committee that Dartmouth House should be kept and developed, it is the view of the remainder of us that Dartmouth House is an albatross around the neck of the Union and that until it is disposed of, we will not be able to expand the Educational and Current Affairs of the Union to the extent that would justify approaching outside interests for significant contributions."

By this time, I was receiving strong reactions from the membership in general and my friends in the Eastern Region in particular to any notion of selling Dartmouth House and I felt impelled to convey this reaction – in no uncertain manner – to the Committee. The loyalty of the membership to their historic HQ led me for the first time to think of Dartmouth House as the St. Peter's of the ESU. (In fact, at the meeting on 19th January, with possibly justified hyperbole, I stated that as you could not conceive of the Catholic Church without St. Peter's, so you could not have an ESU without Dartmouth House. Many theologians might argue with this premise, but it was the premises I was concerned about!)

The growing lobby to save Dartmouth House had distinguished support. By 18th April, Sir Patrick Dean (Chairman of the ESU of the Commonwealth from 1972–83) pledged his support for whatever decision the Committee took, but urged the meeting not to underestimate the importance of Dartmouth House to the prestige and well-being of the ESU. But there were powerful forces ranged against us, and we were running out of time.

However in July, encouragingly, David Emms, Deputy Chairman of the ESU of the Commonwealth stated in a report to the Steering Committee: "My final conclusion is that we should not take the decision now to sell Dartmouth House." Although this gave us a breathing space it was becoming increasingly clear that the tide was turning against us.

The following month, I wrote to Alan Lee Williams, our Director General, mustering my most potent arguments: "I am fully aware that the work of the Union is of greater importance than the bricks and mortar of Dartmouth House, but I am equally sure that the cultural/symbolic significance of the place should not be underestimated. This is just a plea to you to use your influence to encourage the Governors to defer any irrevocable decision before at least the National Council and Regional Chairmen, representing the majority of members, have had a chance to air their views.

"I do feel that once it has been established that the financial controls of the ESU have been tightened and its house put in order there is a good chance of a generous response to a 'Save Dartmouth House' appeal in the USA, in the countries of the Third World, in Europe and from our own membership.

"I should say in conclusion, of course, that whatever the outcome, I, and our members of the Eastern Region, will support you and the ESU wholeheartedly."

The following January, the Governors gloomily concluded that the only solution to the financial problems of the ESU lay in the sale of Dartmouth House. An emergency meeting was immediately called by the Eastern Region Committee, following which I again wrote to the Director General, greatly regretting on behalf of our Committee the course that had been decided upon. The final paragraph of this letter called for the Governors of the Union to "regard the current difficulties as a challenge to more efficiently equip ourselves for service to the wider world in future. 'Without vision, the people perish'."

Alan Lee Williams answered my letter, adding generously: "From many messages received in my office I must conclude that you are probably right."

The debate continued throughout 1985. We lobbied energetically amongst the Governors. It had become clear that if the Headquarters was not to be sold, at least a million pounds would be required for its renovation – and considerably more if our debts were to be reduced, let alone paid off.

The critical meeting was held on 20th August 1986, at which it was resolved that: "All measures necessary for the Union to remain in Dartmouth House shall be taken." The historic resolution was proposed by Sir Donald Tebbit and appropriately seconded by Mr. Robert Sigmon, Chairman of the Pilgrims.

Our struggle had been worthwhile. But although we had won the battle, the fundraising war looked likely to continue for some time, and I was not entirely surprised to be asked by Donald to chair an appeal.

My only previous experience of fund raising had been when I helped Brian Rix raise money for MENCAP, and that successful campaign – it resulted in the endowment of the City Foundation – had involved me in writing just ten letters. The ESU Appeal required me to top and tail more than 8,000!

Any properly organised appeal needs star names and influential supporters. I was fortunate in being able to call upon many of these. The patrons of our appeal included, besides those I have already named in this chapter, the Archbishop of Canterbury, the American Ambassador, Lady Charteris of Amisfield, Winston Churchill M.P., Sir Monty Finniston, Lord Hailsham, Ralph Hammond Innes, Lord Nicholas Hervey, Sir Geoffrey Howe, Lord Lever of Manchester, Lord Montagu of Beaulieu, Sir Randolph Quirk, Sir Shidrath Ramphal, Bernard Weatherill and the Duke of Westminster. The present Lord Rothermere – conscious of course of the close links between Evelyn Wrench and his family – was able to help us with publicity in the Daily

Mail. With Privy Councillors, Companions of Honour and Fellows of the Royal Society to help us, how could we go wrong?

We needed targets, and the first figure that David Hicks – then our acting Director General – plucked out of the air was £750,000, the sum required, he said, to start to put our house in order. HRH The Duke of Edinburgh, President of the ESU, put it a little more delicately in this introduction to our Appeal brochure: "For a great many years, the English-Speaking Union has been demonstrating the value of a common language as a means of encouraging economic progress and of creating better understanding between people all over the world. So much more could be done if only the resources were available."

Prince Philip officially launched our Appeal on 10th March 1987. An Appeal Committee was then set up to mastermind the whole adventurous project. It consisted of Sir Philip Adams, Mrs. Richard Chilton, Mr. Nigel Harrison, Group Captain David Hicks, Mr. Michael von Nagel, Mrs. Stephen Wheatcroft, Major Anthony Gurney, Sir Robin Haydon, Sir Peter Marshall, Mr. Anthony Westnedge and the late the Hon. Kingman Brewster.

Meanwhile, Sir Donald set up an Executive Committee – on which I also sat – to tackle the reorganisation of Dartmouth House, which, by now, we were all determined to preserve and endow for future generations. Perhaps the most significant decision the committee made was to appoint a new Director General, in the person of Rear Admiral Richard Heaslip. He had just retired from a service career – in which his last post was Flag Officer Submarines and NATO's commander Submarines Eastern Atlantic. A move from Admiral to General – Director General to be precise – requires great flexibility and ingenuity and these qualities Dick Heaslip has shown, in no small measure, in leading Dartmouth House staff (now a little better rewarded) into a new era.

Under his direction, Dartmouth House is being completely restored. As the Admiral himself has written: "There is still much to be done, but most of it is now restored to something like the shining splendour of 1885. The Courtyard gleams with flowers and is like a little piece of Paris in London; the Drawing Rooms shine in gold and white; the Walter Hines Page Library is re-opened; the Grand Staircase area is now exquisitely painted with the marble cleaned and the 19th Century ceiling picture restored.

"Those conscious of past problems will be relieved to know that our finances, like the building itself, are now in good shape. Renegotiation of some of our property interests has eliminated all short-term debt, and the money brought in from the Appeal has given us a platform from which to proceed with our work."

Chapter 7

PULLING DOWN THE TOWER OF BABEL

"And who in time knows whither
We may vent the treasures of our tongue?
To what strange shores this again of
our best glory shall be sent
To enrich unknowing nations with our stores?"

Musophilus
Samuel Daniel

"I said it in Hebrew –
I said it in Dutch –
I said it in German and Greek;
But wholly forgot (and it vexes me much)
That English is what you speak!"

The Hunting of the Snark
Lewis Carroll.

On 27th October 1988, the BBC World Service held a seminar called "A Language for the World". It was designed as a way of sharing the thoughts of several distinguished people on the development of the English language – not just how it has developed but how it may; not just how to teach it, but how to use it.

The seminar was opened by HRH the Duke of Edinburgh, who spoke of the value of English as a means of communicating not so much ideas as facts. Commerce, science and technology need a simple form of practical English. Misunderstandings and ambiguities must be avoided; as those who have attended conferences well know, simultaneous translation is not an adequate substitute for a common language. The practical advantages of a universal language would be considerable, but most communities regard their own languages as vital to their national and cultural identity and would see any attempt to impose a common language as a threat.

Esperanto has not, in the view of His Royal Highness, been an unqualified success. At different periods in history different languages have been paramount; Greek in the empire of Alexander the Great, Latin under the Romans, Portuguese, Spanish and English as the empire-builders travelled more and more widely, French for diplomatists and intellectuals, Arabic, Russian and Mandarin Chinese for the huge land-masses who needed to communicate with one another, Swahili and Pidgin English for tradesmen. And now English has become essential for international commerce and communication.

What His Royal Highness was at pains to emphasize was that there are three distinct forms of basic English: a 'cultural' language for literature, poetry and drama, a 'specialised' English for science and technology and a 'technical' English for instructional manuals, air-traffic control and other prosaic but vitally important services. He suggested that it is only cultural English which is seen as a threat by the smaller ethnic communities and that specialised and technical English could (and should) be developed as a sophisticated and unambiguous medium of international communication.

Anthony Burgess spoke on 'cultural' English. The thesis which he developed concerned some of the structuralist ideas of the French linguist and philosopher, Saussure, who stated that language in itself is arbitrary and inert, and that writers, and especially poets, can only animate it by lying. T.S. Eliot begins his masterpiece 'The Waste Land' with the line: "April is the cruellest month", which of course, says Burgess, it is not, or, if it is, only in particular circumstances.

Burgess further subdivides cultural English into 'class one writing' in which the language is transparent and the references easily discerned, and 'class two language' which is opaque, free-structured, and may be observed in the writings of James Joyce, Vladimir Nabokov and Burgess himself. The three novels considered – 'Ulysses', 'Lolita' and 'A Clockwork Orange' – were all 'class two' and condemned as morally dangerous. The more opaque language becomes the more its potential as a subversive influence. Beyond structuralism we move into the world of post-modernism, which proposes that writers do not write, but *are written*, and that their books increasingly belong to a closed world.

Why, one wonders, do these linguistic developments take place within the English language rather than the French? Burgess puts it down to the foreigness of so many of the innovating writers; Eliot, Pound and Henry James – 'class two' writers all – were Americans, James was Irish, Conrad Polish and so on. Whatever the arguments propounded by Burgess there does seem to be something infinitely elastic, endlessly volatile, in the language which permits it to welcome foreign influences and subsume them.

So I believe that the adoption by Third World countries of English as an official language will benefit us all. The traffic is two-way; their cultural possibilities and our linguistic richness are all enhanced.

Amongst other speakers, a witty contribution came from Robert B. Horton, the Chairman of B.P. America. He began by quoting an advertisement put out by the Sony Corporation a few years ago: *"Wanted – Japanese who can swear in English"*, and went on to describe English as a language for doing business in. Four hundred million human beings learn English as babies, he claimed, and 1.36 billion live in countries in which English is the first language of choice. Consequently, almost half all business deals conducted in this over-populated world are concluded in English.

Korean executives in Bangkok doing deals with Italian executives use English. More inhabitants of the Chinese mainland are today learning English than the entire population of the United States. Why? Is it just because Britain and America together create such a vast pool of potential profit? In fact, there are other reasons. Eighty per cent of the world's information stored in computers is in English, and we can be pretty certain that the other 20% will soon go the way of the music cartridge, the black and white television and the Edsel car. There is no arguing with computers. And when the Oxford English Dictionary contains half a million words and those half million words have all been put on a laser disk suitable for feeding into a computer it is no wonder that the English language seems here to stay for those businessmen and businesswomen wedded to their computers.

Then there is the remarkable adaptability of the language, which seems able to survive assaults from every direction, whether newspeak, adspeak, computerspeak, legalese, jargon of every kind, or popular music lyrics. It is, in the hands of the right person, marvellously precise, wonderfully simple. And precision and simplicity are essential in big business if one is to avoid expensive law-suits. In brief, said Mr. Horton, "English is a superb language in which to tell the truth and be understood." And he added a heart-felt wish that "we all do our best to be worthy of this wonderful vehicle for communication, nuance, truth and honourable communion."

Other speakers at the conference included Tim Eggar, Under Secretary of State at the Foreign and Commonwealth Office, Sir Anthony Parsons, former U.K. Permanent Representative to the United Nations and Ngugi wa Thiong'o, the Kenyan novelist and author of 'Decolonising the Mind', who gave his address in KiSwahili, the national language of Kenya, although, I am delighted to report, he was accompanied by his interpreter. An introductory address was given by John Tusa, Managing Director of the BBC World Service.

These men are experts in the use of language; I am not. I hope they will forgive me if, in this chapter, I have drawn – and will draw – on much of what they and others have said to help me marshall my thoughts. My personal belief in the English language is unswerving. Its cultural heritage is unique and it has unique qualities for the communication of ideas and information. This is a vital part of the philosophy of the English-Speaking Union.

The Tower of Babel was built, along with the city which contained it in the Plain of Shinar, by the survivors of the Flood. In those days, according to the Bible, everybody in the world spoke the same language, without even – so far as we are told – regional differences. And the survivors of the Flood said: "Go to, let us build us a city and a tower and let us have its name, lest we be scattered abroad on the face of the whole earth."

They had begun their great building plan when God intervened, disapproving, it seems, of their grand design, and spitefully deciding to "confound their language that they may not understand one another's speech". Not only that but He "scattered them abroad from thence upon the face of all the earth", leaving the city and the tower uncompleted. Why He should have done so is a mystery.

We move rapidly on to 1945 and the creation of the United Nations, where the surviving nations – of a holocaust rather than a flood – built a tower and a city with ambitions not dissimilar to those of the original Babel-builders. (To join the U.N. a nation had to have declared war on the Axis powers before the end of hostilities, which is strange when one considers that today Germany, Italy and Japan are members of the Security Council.) The present U.N. Headquarters – on the island of Manhattan rather than the Plain of Shinar – has two towers, not one, and is entirely complete. Even so, the population of the world would find it hard to fit themselves in. (They could, I am told, all stand shoulder to shoulder on the Isle of Wight, but that would be even more ecologically damaging than the pop festivals of the 1960's!)

When it comes to United Nations language, Article III of the Charter allowed the use of five languages for official business in the Security Council: Chinese, French, Russian, English and Spanish. But for all official documentation only two languages are used, English and French. In the General Assembly, the same five languages are permitted. No African language is employed in any capacity in either the Security Council or the General Assembly. And, partly perhaps because the United

Nations is located within the English-speaking World, English has always predominated.

In 1945, when the British Empire encompassed a quarter of the world's population, there were only 51 member nations. With the break-up of the British Empire a further 50 new members joined. These days, with 151 member nations, the English language is still the most frequently heard in the debating chamber. (The percentages are approximately 27% English, 25% French, 12% Spanish, 12% Arabic, 7% Russian and the remaining 17% in numerous other tongues.) The statistics may not be entirely reliable since, if you speak in a language other than an official or working language, you are required to pay for the simultaneous translation and the circulated documents.

And the English spoken in the U.N. tends to be undistinguished and prosaic, whether for the sake of the poor interpreters, or because the speakers have lost any oratorical flair. Sir Anthony Parsons describes with relish the memorable occasion on which the Head of State of a non-aligned country referred to the Security Council as "this awesome organ", and the English speakers were unable to restrain their raucous laughter.

Officialdom is not just inimical to language, it even changes its meaning. One example: Chapter Seven of the Charter of the U.N. relates to acts of aggression and breaches of the peace. Resolutions passed under this Chapter must be carried out. So that when a war is raging, it is not categorised as a war, to keep it outside the rigours of Chapter Seven. Iran and Iraq were at war for close on ten years, the Arabs and the Israelis have embarked upon a series of wars, there have been some 150 wars since 1945 – but officially they are not wars at all. To save international face in the U.N., delegates do not order or require, they recommend; they do not take measures, they take steps. The English language may have once been a tool of imperialism; it has become a tool of international officialdom.

What we observe at the U.N. is a microcosm of what happens in any august body in which professional people concern themselves with status and hierarchy. In the BBC, executives are known by initials. The ultimate absurdity arose when an engineer of little consequence found himself referred to officially as E.I.E.I.O.! In the courts, barristers confer in a jargon littered with Latin tags, as though it would be unsuitable for the layman to know what is being discussed. In big business, people are paid a salary of £30K – it sounds so much more important than thirty thousand pounds. In each case, language is being used to deceive. Maybe this was what had begun to happen at the Tower of Babel and maybe that was why God took the mysterious decision to confound the bureaucrats and lawyers and executives who were threatening to take control.

It has been well argued – and will continue to be argued – that English is the language of the imperialist oppressor. Certainly, that is how it is seen in many parts of Africa; a language which cannot help but carry implicitly negative images of the conquered race. But to me, this is a complete misunderstanding of how the British Empire allowed itself to be dissolved, leaving behind a rich heritage in many fields – science, medicine, education, business – in which the English language is *non pareil.* It cannot be reiterated too often: in the view of the English-Speaking Union, English is primarily a vehicle of communication.

The English settlers arrived with a sword in one hand and a St. James Bible in the other. More potent than either, it is argued, was the language which they taught in their missionary schools, the language of the text books, the language of an alien culture. But at the same time English was the language of science and the arts, the language – as far as the children could tell – of Holy Scripture. And the language which would open the door to a world as enticing and intriguing as the Holy Grail.

When delegates from these subject nations arrived at the United Nations, what did they find at this international forum for peace and brotherhood? Every language was represented except the language of their own continent. So they learned to become fluent in the language of power, and, by doing so, many felt that they had betrayed in their hearts their countrymen.

Many but not all. Mulk Raj Anand, the Indian savant, argued with the chauvinists amongst his people: "The real English we know was never the language of our conquerors, for it is not they who cherished or brought it into our lives: no, it was the language we ourselves took from the heart of England, not as an act of submission, but through a genuine love of the graces. And even after the last Englishman has left our shores, our affection for it will remain undiminished. And we shall go ourselves, and send our youth, to the sources from which it springs and bring back with us the beauties enshrined in it."

Today, the power of the English language is stronger than it has ever been. Visiting students flock to British Universities (50,000 a year is the current estimate, although this is just half the number who came here to study in 1978) and British academics take up profitable posts at foreign universities. Thus the language in sophisticated forms is disseminated throughout the centres of learning. Publishing houses in Britain publish no fewer than 45,000 titles a year, and almost all of them in English. Goodness knows how many more emanate from American publishers. The under-funded British Council and the under-funded World Service of the BBC do remarkably under their straitened circumstances to export British culture to those who wish to be exposed to it.

The status of the English language in the British Asian colonies has a chequered history. During the struggle for independence in India and Sri Lanka, the speaking of English was regarded as disreputable and those Asians who insisted on it were categorised as lackeys of imperialism. In India, the slogan was: "Banish English!"; in Sri Lanka: "Sinhala only!" In 1956, English was removed as the link language in Sri Lanka. But in the meanwhile passions have cooled. Many Indian scholars make a distinction between what is referred to distastefully as "King Emperor's English" and the English of Shakespeare and Milton. The imperialist's English was not only a limited and demeaned version of the true language but it was very inadequately taught. The English text-books contained versions of history which no Indian or Sri Lankan could possibly recognize. Disinformation was the fashion. The Babu caricature of the Indian minor government official struggling to master English manners and idioms and only succeeding in making himself ridiculous was unfortunately only too accurate. Such hybrid figures were humiliated by the British and derided by their countrymen. The true usefulness of English in India was to provide common ground between, say, a civil servant from Tamil Nadu and an M.P. from Uttar Pradesh, and in Sri Lanka between a Sinhalese administrator and a Tamil librarian.

In 1983, two years after the founding of the English-Speaking Union of Sri Lanka, in an historic speech before Parliament, ex-President Jayawardene announced that: "Sinhala and Tamil are the media of instruction and Sinhala is the official language. Tamil is a national language and the elevation of English to a similar position will enable it to act as a link language between Sinhalese and Tamil-speaking people and the international world." The restoration of English to its proper position was long overdue and was particularly welcomed by Commonwealth Secretary-General Shridath (Sonny) Ramphal, who declared: "English is the Commonwealth's precious legacy of an imperfect past."

Today, the educated Sinhalese would not regard the English language as a foreign language; it is as much his or her birthright as that of someone living in Manchester or Surrey. The major newspapers are in English, and most major institutions on the island have developed examinations in English for their staff. But without standardisation this has been a haphazard process, and it fell to the ESU to develop a graded system of English testing with seven stages of excellence, much like music grades.

As in Sri Lanka, so in the rest of Asia, so in the rest of the world.

When English lessons were first introduced on the Chinese radio, their tremendous popularity was self-evident. All work stopped in the compound of the British Embassy as the Chinese staff huddled round their radios, apparently repeating: "In the kitchen, I see one rifle, two rifles, three rifles."

The British staff never did learn the significance of rifles in a Chinese kitchen, but they were delighted when strangers came up to them in the street to try out their first few words of English. The anonymous throngs were immediately transformed into collections of individuals, any one of whom had the potential to become a friend through the exchange of ideas.

Surely this is the heart of the matter: the ability of individual men and women from an infinite variety of cultural backgrounds to understand each other across political as well as geographical frontiers.

I am convinced there is a strong connection between the wider peace that the world has known over the last 40 years and the enormous development of media technology over that same period. During the Falklands crisis, for instance, when interviews with English-speaking Argentine citizens were shown on television news bulletins, they had an undeniable influence on public opinion throughout the anglophone world and played a part in ensuring, as far as the British were concerned, that a purely military confrontation did not develop into a far more serious breakdown of relations between our two peoples.

It may be a surprise to some – especially newer members of the ESU – to learn that English as a language has not always been central to our work. The name 'English-Speaking Union' had originally defined the areas in which the organisation operated. As recently as 1975, HRH The Duke of Edinburgh pointed out that whenever he travelled abroad, he found many peoples trying to speak English, not always successfully. He asked the ESU whether it was not the natural body to do something about it.

In a preface to a significant new work entitled: 'ESU Framework' by Brendan J. Carroll and Richard West (Longman 1989), David Hicks describes what happened next. An English language committee was formed of distinguished professors and English teachers under Prince Philip's chairmanship. Two annual competitions – one for unpublished and one for published works – were initiated. So too were a series of conferences, lectures and research projects aimed at creating new kinds of basic English for use amongst seamen, airmen and scientists. With sponsorship from Reed International, David brought together a small team to work under the banner of the ESU; the intention was to devise some kind of yardstick for measuring standards of English. It did this with considerable success; at least seven of the major examining bodies cooperated and students throughout the world will find an examination system considerably safer and more rational than any that preceded it.

If evidence is needed as to the extraordinary influence wielded by the English language at the end of the twentieth century, one only has to consider the Salman Rushdie affair. A few years ago it is highly improbable that a book written in English by an author living in England, an author moreover with no political reputation, could have so offended the Islamic people that death threats would have been issued against the author, the publisher and those who spoke out publicly on the author's behalf; that trade between Britain and Iran should have been halted and that diplomatic relations should have been broken off; that dozens should have died in riots. Truly the pen (or perhaps I should say the word processor!) is mightier than the sword, and when the pen writes in the English language the whole world takes note. It seems inevitable that, as on the Plain of Shinar, it will not be long before the whole world speaks with a single voice – whether that voice is the voice of colonial oppression or the voice of Keats and Shakespeare, the voice of science and technology or the voice of faceless officialdom. Capable of infinite subtleties or deliberate deceits, the English language will be the inspiration and the despair of the whole brotherhood and sisterhood of man.

Speaking at the Guildhall at a luncheon given by the City of London to mark her Silver Jubilee, Her Majesty The Queen said: "It is easy enough to define what the Commonwealth is not, indeed this is quite a popular pastime! But from my own experience I know something of what it is. It is like an iceberg, except that it's not cold! The tip is represented by the occasional meetings of heads of government – and right at the base of the iceberg, the part that keeps the rest afloat is friendship and communication, largely in the English language."

I can do no better than to echo those words.

Chapter 8

THE ASIAN CONNECTION

"Asia is not going to be civilised after the methods of the West. There is too much Asia and she is too old."

The Man Who Was
Rudyard Kipling

Dr. Amerasinghe and I felt not a little excitement as we set out for Delhi. We had been invited by some friends of the good doctor, who were eager to start a Delhi branch of the ESU. As a result of Sir Evelyn Wrench's visits to India there has been a network of like-minded souls with branches in such important centres as Bombay, Calcutta and Poona. However, there was one mysterious and serious omission; for some reason nobody had thought to open an ESU branch in the capital.

We arrived at dead of night from Sri Lanka via Madras. It was bitterly cold and the airport was in chaos – which made the creature comforts of the Oberoi Hotel all the more welcome when eventually we arrived there, in the early hours of the morning.

After a few hours sleep, a good breakfast and a walk through the beautifully tended gardens, I was eager to meet the group which was gathering in my suite to discuss the formation of the Delhi branch. The group included Mr. B.P. Nigam, a lawyer and civil servant, Mrs. Ayesha Sultan, a journalist and social worker, the Hon. R.P. Sinha, former Secretary General of the Congress Party, Mr. Ratansing Rajda, former member of Lok Sabha, and Mr. S. Pandey, a well-known Delhi advocate.

Our discussions continued for two days during which all present expressed enormous enthusiasm for a Delhi branch. It became clear that there would be support, too, from the Delhi public. By the end of our second day of talks, it was unanimously decided that we should go ahead. It was with great satisfaction and confidence that I was able to hand over the chair to Mr. Pandey, who had done much sterling work for the United Nations Association and was the most obvious candidate to act as the co-ordinating President. Mr. Ratansing Rajda was elected Chairman with Mr. B.P. Nigam and Mr. R.P. Sinha as Vice-Chairmen. Mrs. Ayesha Sultan was elected Secretary.

The Times of India gave front-page coverage to the formation of the Delhi branch on 6th February under the heading: "English-Speaking Union branch in the capital". The report went on to say: "After speaking, reading and writing English for more than a century and a half, Delhi has now for the first time a branch of the English-Speaking Union."

To celebrate, Mr. Rajda gave a small luncheon at the Gymkhana Club for Dr. Amerasinghe and myself and a few members of the newly-formed committee. I was much amused, over a glass of port, to hear a refined brigadier mutter: "I hear women are now allowed in the St. James Clubs – what are things coming to in England?" There is no such egalitarianism in the Gymkhana Club!

Unfortunately, I was unable to be present for the formal opening of the branch which did not take place until a year later on 19th January 1987. This was because it was felt – and rightly so in my opinion – that a great deal of groundwork should be done in order to give the branch a strong and lasting base. Changes took place within the committee and the leadership to allow those with most time and influence to occupy key positions. A programme was planned stressing, not inappropriately, the literary aspect of our work.

Eventually the day for the inauguration arrived. The meeting was held at the YMCA with Mr. Escuadero, the US Consul, officiating. Mr. Nigam spoke of the disaffection caused by the lack of a common language. Mrs. Sultan emphasized that, important as the issue of language was, the true aim of the ESU was to further the aims of peace, friendship and international understanding. With 70,000 members and 160 branches throughout the world it was uniquely placed to do so. After speeches by Mr. Sinha, Belinda Norman-Butler (representing the National Council for England and Wales) and Mr. Pandey, Mr. Escuadero gave his address. In this, he argued that it was essential that the translation system currently used at the U.N. must be replaced and that one common language should replace the mayhem. He remarked on the coincidence that the date of the inauguration was the birthday of the late Martin Luther King and concluded that without the English language, King would not have been so powerfully influenced by the ideas of Mahatma Gandhi. (Gandhi wrote both 'Young India' and 'Experiments in Truth' in English.)

I was particularly glad that Mrs. Norman-Butler was able to be present on this important occasion. Few have done more for the ESU in England and Wales and even fewer of our members know Delhi as well.

1987 proved to be not only a busy year for Dr. Amerasinghe and myself, but also a successful one. In early February, we set out for Nepal at the invitation of Mr. N.B. Bajracharya, the respected leading Nepalese educationalist, who had suggested donating a school to the ESU, which he envisaged could become the basis of a Nepalese branch. It seemed that a growing number of ESU enthusiasts had heard of our reception and subsequent success in Delhi.

The most vivid description of the ESU school at Kathmandu comes from one of our student-teachers, Rachel Steward, who taught there in 1986: "My host, the principal of the school, took us to his centre. I was installed in a beautiful third floor room of the school, overlooking the mighty Himalayan foothills.

"From seven-year-olds to twelve-year-olds, my pupils were a delight. It was a 'good morning, miss' and a 'good evening, miss', always with a most graceful bow. After sessions of singing, dancing and teaching, to retire to my room overlooking the serene Pagoda Swayambhumi was joy unutterable. Late evening walks to the Tibetan temple and encounters with gangs of monkeys were nerve-tingling but delightful.

"The school's fame seems to have already spread to Europe and America. Both because of its humanitarian appeal and the fact that its principal, Mr.Bajracharya, is a well-known authority on Badriyana Buddhism considered older than even the Greater or Lesser Wheels, it draws teachers and visitors from the Occident. Beside me on the staff were an Austrian and an American girl.

"Kathmandu Valley is a tourist's paradise, a souvenir hunter's dream and an archaeologist's evocation! Food, however, was to me a problem. The heavy spices caused havoc with my stomach. It would have been wise had I been broken into it gradually. But I was loath to refuse the colourful repast when it was laid before me by my genial hosts.

"Speaking frankly, food soured my stay. However, I lived through my assignment and bid a tearful farewell to my little friends, who to my utter consternation kissed my feet in anguish. Respect for teachers is profound in Nepal and, I have reason to think, all over Asia; and knowledge for English an unquenchable thirst.

"I returned to my work at the ESU Headquarters in Sri Lanka via two glorious days in Bangkok. Sri Lanka with its palm-fringed shores and spicy garlic smells, its quick-tanning sun is for me dearer far than Nepal. Now in England I sometimes reproach myself; 'the sly slow hours do not determinate the dateless limit of my dear exile'."

In Delhi, the main interest of the founders of the ESU had been the cultural and commercial impact of the English language; in Kathmandu we were back to basics. There is no great tradition of English culture there but there is an unslaking thirst for it. It was fortunate that two of our Nepalese founder members were an educationalist and a keen exponent of English. The good doctor and I remained in Nepal for several days – long enough to see a committee formed under the Chairmanship of Mr. Bajracharya and the Presidency of Rabi Charan Shresha, a leading political figure.

Before we left England, Anthony Westnedge had very generously arranged to donate a case of Johnny Walker whisky for Dr. Amerasinghe and myself to present to His Majesty King Birenda. Who can say whether there was any significant connection between the presentation to Nepal's delightful (and English-educated) Monarch and his subsequent agreement to become patron of the ESU of Nepal?

Before reluctantly departing the Kingdom we found time to see something of the wild open spaces at the bottom of awe-inspiring mountains with remarkable, indigenous flora and fauna. One of the highlights of my trip was a visit to the Royal Botanical Gardens in the laboratories of which I inspected a remarkable crawling stick-plant – half-plant and half-animal – and no, I had not been consuming a bottle of the King's whisky!

On 16th March 1987, members of the ESU from most of the South Asian Council for Regional Co-operation countries met at Delhi's Hotel Vivek to form a cultural council which could consolidate and strengthen existing ties of friendship through the medium of English. The participants were India, Sri Lanka, Nepal, Pakistan and the Maldive Islands (where already, there was a growing interest in our work, but as yet no branch), Bangladesh and Bhutan, whose delegates were merely observers but who will soon have ESU branches of their own.

It was clear that the desire for a working knowledge of the English language had become a mass movement. Politicians ignored it at their peril. In Sri Lanka in the late 1950's, an ambitious young man could gain political credibility by plugging the anti-English line. Now the reverse applies. And not only in Sri Lanka. English is no longer regarded as the prerogative of the upper and middle classes. At the ESU teaching seminars, university lecturers, lawyers and accountants, sit cheek by jowl with taxi-drivers, nurses, clerks and house-maids. Everybody needs to speak English; but the educational systems cannot cope and most governments are too busy with the ever-present problems of terrorism and too impoverished by them to provide funds for the teaching of English.

Why cannot this valuable service be provided by the British Council? First, because there remains a lurking suspicion that such an organisation represents some of the negative aspects of the imperialist past, and secondly, because quite simply the British Council classes are far too expensive for the average purse. The ESU, on the other hand, is a people's movement and the fees are modest. A typical student is more at home with our rough wooden desks, our impoverished equipment and our ill-ventilated rooms than with the spacious grandeur of the British Council.

After an opening address by the convenor, Mr. Pandey, Mr. Rajda announced that I had been unanimously elected President of the Council. He recalled how when India needed to appoint its first Governor-General it turned not to an Indian but to an Englishman, the late Lord Louis Mountbatten. The process was being repeated with me. It was a proud moment, and I would be a hypocrite if I did not acknowledge it as such.

Mr. Rajda added that the Sri Lankan branch was the best organised in the region and that it had therefore been chosen as the Headquarters of the Council, and that Dr. Amerasinghe was to be the first Secretary General of the South Asia Council. This too was excellent news.

As I glanced at the officials of the South Asia ESU it was

impossible not to be impressed by the wealth of talent and influence represented. The patrons included the Hon. Dr. Nissanka Wijeyeratne, the Hon. R.P. Sinha, Ahmed E.H. Jaffer (President of the ESU Pakistan), Prince Mohsin Ali Khan of Hyderabad, the Hon. Mohamed Zahir Hussain (Minister of Education in the Maldives) and the Hon. Marich Mansingh Shrestra (Prime Minister of Nepal).

My Vice-President was Mr. Rajda, and I recently had the pleasure of welcoming two further Vice-Presidents, Mr. Klaus Reimann, a leading engineer and interpreter from Hamburg and Princess Usha devi Rathore. And I had David Hicks as my consultant on the English language and educational affairs.

Once our meetings had been concluded, I was delighted to have a few days free to explore what must surely be one of the world's most fascinating cities. But moved as we both were by the astonishing architecture and picturesque gardens, my outstanding memory is of standing before Ghandi's tomb. As Dr. Amerasinghe and I stood in silent tribute to the memory of one of Asia's greatest sons, I recollected the astonishing single-minded and visionary dedication which had enabled Ghandi to achieve such miracles. The following words are carved on the tomb:

THE GANDHI TALISMAN

Recall the face of the
Poorest and the most
Helpless man whom you
May have seen and ask
Yourself if the step you
Contemplate is going to be
Of any use to him. Will
He be able to gain anything

By it? Will it restore him
To a control over his own
Life and destiny? In other
Words, will it lead to
Swaraj or self-rule for the
Hungry and also spiritually
Starved millions of our
Countrymen? Then you will
Find your doubts and
Yourself melting away.

Sir Donald Tebbit, during his inaugural remarks at the 1986 ESU World Members Conference in Edinburgh, referred to my extensive travels in Asia and the founding of the new branches and surprised me by referring to me as the St. Paul of the ESU. This flattering description was in my mind when, in January 1988, Dr. Amerasinghe and I set out once again on our travels. This time, our destination was the extreme south of South Asia, the Maldive Islands.

I had prepared the ground. Dr. Nissanka Wijeyerantne, the Sri Lankan Minister of Justice, had introduced me to the Maldivian Ambassador to Sri Lanka – who had immediately warmed to the idea of forming an ESU of the Maldives and had telephoned his President, His Excellency Maumoon Abdul Gayoom, who shared his enthusiasm.

As Dr. Amerasinghe and I sped towards the capital, Male, by speedboat, we were accompanied by two dark-eyed, dusky girls and I could not help but wonder if St. Paul had been as lucky. But I was to receive an unpleasant shock. As soon as we had moored in the small port, the local girls disappeared – taking our passports with them. Were we to be prisoners forever on these remote, sun-soaked islands? Sadly, we were not. We could only justify staying long enough to establish the new ESU branch under the direction of its Chairman, the Minister of Education, Mohamed Zahir Hussain.

Education in the Maldives was traditionally the responsibility of Moslem leaders and mainly consisted of religious studies based on the Koran. The language was Arabic and teaching informal – mostly taking place in private homes where a teacher was available.

There was a major change in the educational system with the introduction of the first secondary school – initially limited to boys – which opened in Male in 1927. (Girls *were* later admitted; their studies confined to the evenings.)

Thereafter, schools developed throughout the islands. They were known as *Makthambs*, where religious education continued to predominate, the other principal subject being arithmetic. And when primary schools – called *Madhrassa* – were also formed, history, too, took its place on the timetable.

President Gayoom has emphasised the importance of education for all and has given government funds to assist the schools. But funds are short. English schools are few – but in great demand – and the government is interested in joint ventures with private foundations to establish many more.

As in Nepal, it soon became apparent that the main preoccupation and principal activity of the Maldivian ESU was to be the teaching of English. But the shortage of qualified teachers was bound to be a problem and the words of our President, HRH Prince Philip, came once more into my mind: "So much more could be done, if only the resources were available."

To date, we have laid the foundations of the ESU edifice in South Asia, but I am convinced that as Asia grows during the next decade into a powerful economic base, so the ESU will grow with it, expanding its influence and increasing its usefulness.

What lessons have we learned in establishing these successful ESU branches? Most importantly, the necessity for the right person in the right place at the right time. To Buddhists, this is Karma – the only way. And the right person needs to be somebody local, who knows the territory. No permanent and effective branch will be formed by outsiders nor by directives from distant committees. I could never have succeeded in setting up the ESU in Sri Lanka, for instance, without Dr. Amerasinghe, who had huge influence within and knowledge of the country.

Then I believe it to be essential that we show an understanding of local circumstances and a respect for local traditions. This holds true whether one is dealing with a branch in Norfolk, in Nepal or in the USA. (Incidentally, it is my belief that the need for the teaching of the English language is as great in America – with its continuing influx of foreigners and its widespread ethnic languages – as anywhere in the world.) We must continue to emphasize that we have no desire to impose an alien culture on an indigenous population. On the contrary, we must stress the vital importance of using English as a method of both cultures learning more of one another.

There is also the significant matter of charitable status. Once this has been granted, we are seen to be respectable; furthermore, we are the vehicle for tax-efficient donations from many commercial enterprises who appreciate and support our language and exchange schemes and who wish to offer practical help.

Finally, we need to build up in each centre a strong administrative system and an expanding team of willing volunteers. No-one is indispensable, and one must always look to the volunteers to provide likely candidates for the succession. We need the leaders of the future and we need a loyal body of supporters to stand behind them.

Above all, no matter how important the peripheral activities, we should never lose sight of the ESU's principal aims: the promotion of the English language, the provision of a platform for continuing debate and a forum for human friendship in dignity.

At the time of writing – July 1989 – it is encouraging to watch the South Asia Council developing slowly but surely. It was agreed at the inaugural meeting in Delhi that the headquarters should be in Colombo – an appropriate choice, since this is where our Asian initiative started, and a practical one, since the Sri Lanka ESU has the only permanent staff on the continent. The Council has its own office situated in our new Colombo centre.

There has been active support for the South Asia Association ESU, especially in London. On 26th September 1988, I presided at a reception at Dartmouth House, attended by a glittering array of guests, including diplomats, politicians and businessmen, the High Commissioner of Sri Lanka, the Ambassadors of Nepal and Pakistan, Lords Glenarthur, Sudeley, Montagu of Beaulieu, and many others. Dr. Amerasinghe, who came to London specially for the occasion gave the address, and the Hon. J. Sinclair Armstrong, Chairman of the American ESU responded. It was encouraging to have the leader of the largest ESU region in the world supporting the smallest – so far – and newest region.

It is an advantage that two patrons of the South Asia Council spend much of their time in London. Princess Usha devi Rathore, the grand-daughter of the late Sir Uday Chand Mahtab, Maharajadhiraja Bahadur of Burdwan, who led the ESU in Calcutta for many years. Thus a link is formed between the original Indian ESU branches, forged by Sir Evelyn Wrench, and the new and vigorous ESU era into which we have entered. At her first International Council meeting, Princess Usha said the following: "I feel that the ESU has a special role to play in this present day when the world is going through a period of great transition. Mankind is going into the next phase of evolution, when he must stop thinking in tribal terms and acquire a more global perspective.

"With the advent of modern telecommunications, satellite and computer links, it is possible for information to reach all members of the human race almost instantaneously.

"My father is Rajput and my mother is Bengali and we lived in Bombay where the regional tongues are Gujerati and Marathi, so at home we spoke to each other in English! English helps to break down so many language barriers between the peoples of various nations, and so promotes understanding and mutual respect for each other's cultures."

So impressed was Francis Pym, the Chairman of the ESU of the Commonwealth, that he immediately asked for a copy of the Princess's speech.

Prince Nawab Mir Mohsin Ali Khan belongs to the internationally known and highly respected family of the Nizam of Hyderabad. He has provided not only an important link between the U.K. and India but another between India and Pakistan. He has supported the Council from its inception and has always been willing to address meetings on the South Asia work. He is currently President of both the British Muslim and Christian Society and of the British Muslim Islamic Council.

I can mention Pakistan and not mention our oldest – I hope he will forgive me – ESU leader in South Asia, Ahmed Jaffer, whose services to the ESU have been rewarded with a well-deserved CBE.

Asia in general – and, I believe, South Asia in particular – has a very bright future. In economic terms, whether one looks at leisure, tourism, social capital, infrastructure, consumption or a host of other indicators, the region is firmly behind Western nations and, now possessing the wherewithal, very keen to catch up.

The region has close historic ties with – of all Western nations – the United Kingdom, and despite the popular Empire-bashing of the 1960's and 70's, more and more Britons are entering into partnership with Asians, in a vast and diverse range of activities.

Sri Lankans, particularly, are natural allies, for they respect the British democratic traditions and practice what they have largely made their own. In the early days, they had discovered that the British, being themselves an independent and insular people, were not by nature imperialistic. They had seemed more interested in planting settlements of their own people in unoccupied spaces of the Earth – and they were interested in trade. It was as a by-product of those interests that they found themselves involved in controlling a number of countries which possessed their own populations and cultures – and they never knew quite what to do about it.

As Sir Oliver Goonetilleke, former Governor-General of Ceylon, observed: "They readily, and on the whole successfully, exercised a paternal sway over the peoples in a primitive stage of social development, but they were not happy at dealing with those who had passed that stage."

Long ago, the Romans conquered Britain, attempting to assimilate the people as they colonised and Romanised their land. Their language, now dead, represented loss of national identity and loss of freedom.

Today, throughout South Asia, English represents opportunity – it provides a key to the door of the future for all and moreover, a bridge across the ethnic divide.

The major problems faced in this new situation by all South Asian countries are shared.

First, there is the inability of everyday educational systems to cope with the colossal demand. Next, the fact that Governments alone are unable to meet the ever-growing needs; private enterprise must play a part, especially since government funds which might once have been able to meet the demand for English schools are now dwindling, in the face of mounting expenditure to quell terrorism. Finally, the lack of experienced English teachers is felt throughout the sub-continent; if the demand from the masses for "spoken English" is not met, there could be a negative reaction and deep resentment.

The English-Speaking Union is now flourishing in South Asia. The danger is that we might miss this great opportunity to use English to foster and promote international goodwill and understanding.

As I finish writing, I cannot help but recollect Derek Neville and that dinner in Itteringham Mill. If I had never read Derek's poetry, our friendship would not have developed and he would certainly never have presented me with the mysterious "message from Goethe". Would I have become involved so passionately with the future of the English language and that troubled but beautiful little island so full of ancient reservoirs and brilliant sapphires?

One thing is certain. The message holds true:

What you can do – or think you can – Begin it!
Boldness hath genius, power and magic in it.
Only engage, and then the mind grows heated
Begin!
And soon your task shall be completed.

Perhaps not entirely true. Will the task soon be completed? I doubt it. And after all, what would I do with myself if it were?

Michael Wynne-Parker
Norfolk, England
July 1989

APPENDIX

THE ESU OF SRI LANKA

Patron
H.E., The President of Sri Lanka

President
Dr. T.P. Amerasinghe

Chairman
Mr. J. Asitha Perera

Appeal Chairman
Mr. Michael Wynne-Parker
President: The Council of the ESU of South Asia
Governor: ESU of the Commonwealth
Vice-President: ESU of Sri Lanka

Appeal Committee
Mr. Abdul Ameer
Dr. T.P. Amerasinghe
Mrs. Lester Cooray
Mr. Ruwan Fonseka
Mrs. Krishni Jayawardena
Mrs. N. V. Jayawardene
Mr. J. Asitha Perera
Hon. Justice H. Rodrigo
Mr. Nimalsri Silva
Mr. A. Hathy Suliaman
Mr. Ajith Tudawe
Mr. Larksman Wijewardene

Appeal Patrons

Hon. J.R. Jayawardene, Former President of Sri Lanka
Dr. M. Barccani-Dunston
Dr. Arthur C. Clarke
The Rt. Rev. Swithin Fernando
Mr. N.U. Jayawardena
Dr. M.C.M. Kaleel
Hon. M.H. Mohammad
Mr. H.E. Peiris
H.E., Sir Shridath Ramphal
Mrs. Loranee Senaratne
Hon. Dr. Nissanka Wijeyeratne
Collins Publishers
Mr. Lester Fonseka
Lord Nicholas Hervey
Hon. Bakeer Markar
Sir John Nicholas
The Ven. Piyadassi Maha Thero
Hon. C. Rajadurai
The Ven. Walpola Rahula
Hon. F. Sharvananda
Hon. S. Thondaman
Mr. Anton Wijegoonewardena
Mr. Ranjan Wijemanne

THE SOUTH ASIA COUNCIL OF THE ENGLISH-SPEAKING UNION

Patrons

Hon. Dr. Nissanka Wijeyeratne
Hon. R. P. Sinha
Ahmed E. H. Jaffer
Prince Moshin Ali Kahn of Hyderabad
Hon. Mohammad Hussein
Hon. Marich Mansingh Shrestra
Princess Usha devi Rathore
Mr. Klaus Reimann

President

Mr. Michael Wynne-Parker

Vice-President

Mr. Ratnasingh Rajda

Chairman

Mr. S. D. Pandey

Secretary-General

Dr. T. P. Amerasinghe

CONSULTANT ON ENGLISH LANGUAGE AND EDUCATIONAL AFFAIRS

Mr. David Hicks MBE

SOUTH ASIA COUNCIL OF THE ENGLISH-SPEAKING UNION

Constituent Member Countries

India – full member
Sri Lanka – full member
Nepal – full member
Pakistan – full member
Maldive Islands – full member
Bangladesh – representative only
Bhutan – representative only

Headquarters:
c/o The English-Speaking Union of Sri Lanka
314/2 Galle Road
Kollopitiya
Colombo 3
Sri Lanka

INDEX